KT-382-315

DK EYEWITNESS TOP 10 TRAVEL GUIDES

DUBROVNIK
& THE DALMATIAN COAST

ROBIN AND JENNY MCKELVIE

Left **Excursion boat, Cavtat** Right **Fish platter, Nostromo, Split**

LONDON, NEW YORK,
MELBOURNE, MUNICH AND DELHI
www.dk.com

Produced by DP Services,
C7, Old Imperial Laundry
Warriner Gardens, London SW11 4XW

Reproduced by Colourscan, Singapore
Printed and bound in China by Leo
Paper Products Ltd

First published in Great Britain in 2006
by Dorling Kindersley Limited
80 Strand, London WC2 R 0RL
A Penguin Company

Reprinted with revisions 2008

**Copyright 2006, 2008 ©
Dorling Kindersley Limited, London**

A CIP catalogue record is available from
the British Library.

ISBN: 978-1-40532-129-7

Within each Top 10 list in this book, no
hierarchy of quality or popularity is
implied. All 10 are, in the editor's
opinion, of roughly equal merit.

Contents

Top 10 of Dubrovnik & the Dalmatian Coast

The information in this DK Eyewitness Top 10 Travel Guide is checked regularly.
Every effort has been made to ensure that this book is as up-to-date as possible at the time of
going to press. Some details, however, such as telephone numbers, opening hours, prices,
gallery hanging arrangements and travel information are liable to change. The publishers
cannot accept responsibility for any consequences arising from the use of this book, nor for
any material on third party websites, and cannot guarantee that any website address in this
book will be a suitable source of travel information. We value the views and suggestions of
our readers very highly. Please write to: Publisher, DK Eyewitness Travel Guides,
Dorling Kindersley, 80 Strand, London, Great Britain WC2R 0RL.

Left **Onofrio's Fountain, Stradun, Dubrovnik** Right **River Čikola, Krka National Park**

Left **Old town, Dubrovnik** Right **Croatian National Theatre, Split**

TOP 10 OF DUBROVNIK & THE DALMATIAN COAST

🔟 Highlights

Whether you visit for the sun, the sailing, the scenery, or some of the freshest seafood you'll find anywhere, the Dalmatian coast is quite simply one of Europe's most stunning escapes. Long stretches of glorious shoreline are framed between striking limestone mountains and the azure waters of the Adriatic, where hundreds of islands, inhabited and uninhabited, await exploration. The coastline is punctuated by a series of lively towns and cities, in which the region's long and eclectic history comes alive in wonderfully preserved "old cores" that are no mere museum-pieces, but vibrant, bustling hubs of activity – nowhere more so than Dubrovnik, a UNESCO World Heritage Site now returned to its former splendour after the siege of the early 1990s.

1 Old City Walls, Dubrovnik
For centuries, the remarkable old city walls have afforded Dubrovnik protection. Today they allow visitors a bird's-eye view of one of Europe's most impressive cities *(see pp8–9)*.

2 Stradun, Dubrovnik
Along its polished expanse, Dubrovnik's elegant pedestrianized main thoroughfare boasts a wealth of churches, palaces, shops, fountains and pavement cafés *(see pp10–13)*.

3 Rector's Palace, Dubrovnik
Under the Republic of Ragusa, the city's figurehead presided here, amidst a flurry of Gothic and Renaissance architecture. This impressive palace has now been reinvented as a museum and cultural venue *(see pp14–15)*.

4 Korčula Town
It may or may not be the birthplace of Marco Polo, but Korčula Town is simply sublime, set on its own peninsula, framed by sea and mountains. Its cathedral is one of the most charming ecclesiastical buildings in the Adriatic *(see pp16–17)*.

Preceding pages **View of rooftops from Dubrovnik city walls**

Trogir
Set on its own island, this perfectly preserved old city shimmers with churches, palaces and one of Europe's most striking cathedrals, whose beauty is recognized by UNESCO *(see pp18–19).*

Krka National Park
Established to protect the middle and lower reaches of the River Krka, this idyllic natural playground of lakes, waterfalls and waterways near Šibenik attracts small kids and big kids alike *(see pp20–21).*

Diocletian's Palace, Split
The palatial, UNESCO-World-Heritage-listed retirement home of Emperor Diocletian forms the frenetic heart of the dashing Mediterranean city of Split *(see pp22–5).*

Kornati National Park
This necklace of largely uninhabited islands strung out in the Adriatic has become a paradise for sailors, and for those looking to escape the strains and stresses of modern life *(see pp26–7).*

Cathedral of St James, Šibenik
Now fully restored since its shelling in 1991, this splendid cathedral is one of Europe's finest – and another UNESCO-World-Heritage-listed gem *(see pp28–9).*

Zadar Old Town
This proud survivor is now back to its lively best, with Slavic culture meeting Roman remnants on a striking Adriatic peninsula *(see pp30–31).*

🔟 Old City Walls, Dubrovnik

Dubrovnik's voluminous city walls, up to 12 m (39 ft) thick and 25 m (82 ft) high in places, are a stunning site. A cradle of stone, they helped to protect one of the most perfectly preserved medieval cities in Europe, as well as safeguarding the independence of the city-state for centuries. Running from the steep cliffs to the north through to the Adriatic in the south, they proved an impenetrable barrier to pirates and potential conquerors, until the keys to the gates were finally handed over to the French on 31 January 1808, and the Republic of Dubrovnik (or Ragusa, to use its former name) came to an end.

Steps up to the track along the top of the walls

🄐 **Buža**, perched outside the southern walls overlooking the Adriatic and Lokrum, is a bar well worth seeking out. No food or fancy service here, but refreshing drinks and stunning views. From the Jesuit Church, follow the "cold drinks" sign.

🄑 Be sure to carry plenty of water in the warmer months, as the only place on the walls where liquid refreshment is available is at the drinks counter on the southern flank.

• Map G4
• Access from the Stradun (next to the Pile Gate), Svetog Dominika and Kneza Damjana. Open 9am–6:30pm daily. Adm charge 50kn (children 20kn; audio handsets also available)
• Maritime Museum: 020 323 904. Open May–Oct: 9am–6pm daily; Nov–Apr: 9am–2pm daily. Adm charge 35kn (children/students 15kn; groups 20kn)

Top 10 Sights
1. Pile Gate
2. Minčeta Fort
3. Ploče Gate
4. Revelin Fort
5. Rooftops
6. St John's Fort
7. Maritime Museum
8. Drinks Counter
9. Bokar Fort
10. Boat Trip

Pile Gate
This grand western entrance to the Old City leads, via a drawbridge, down on to the Stradun. Look out for the figure of Dubrovnik's patron saint, St Blaise, above the gate and, a little further on, for a more modern depiction by Ivan Meštrović.

Minčeta Fort
North of the Pile Gate, steep steps lead up to an impressive fort *(below)*. Views at sunset from this 15th-century bastion justify the exertion to reach it.

Ploče Gate
The bridge leading to the Ploče Gate *(above)*, on the eastern walls, offers new arrivals tantalizing glimpses of the city and the old port.

Revelin Fort
Close to the eastern walls stands this sturdy 16th-century fortress, now used for music and dance events in summer.

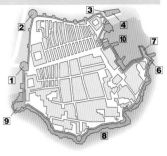

Rooftops
5 The legacy of the 1991–92 siege is evident from the stretch of wall around the old port. From here the contrast between the charming, original roof tiles and the newer replacements, imported from France and Slovenia, is easy to see.

Pile Gate

Bokar Fort
9 This Renaissance fort, designed by Michelozzo Michelozzi, watches over the city's original port. From here the Lovrijenac fortress is visible across the water.

St John's Fort
6 This fortification *(right)* protected the old port from advancing enemy ships and was, in its time, right at the cutting edge of military technology. Begun in the 14th century, additions were being made well into the 16th century.

Drinks Counter
8 On the southern flank of the walls there is an unassuming drinks stand with outdoor seating. This is a fine spot to rest on a hot day and admire the hulking fortifications and the island of Lokrum.

Boat Trip
10 For a completely different perspective of Dubrovnik's walls, join a tour boat or hire a local water taxi (both leave from the old port) and skirt around the base of the city *(left)*, where the Adriatic swishes against the rocks and the ramparts soar menacingly upward.

Maritime Museum
7 Part of St John's Fortress is a museum *(see p40)*, that sheds light on the Republic of Ragusa's rich and eclectic maritime heritage. The exhibits include a large collection of model ships, sepia photographs of the port and historic maps.

Libertas
Dubrovnik's daunting city walls are just part of the reason why the Republic of Ragusa enjoyed centuries of independence, at a time when the Venetians and Turks were vying for territory all around the Adriatic. Machiavelli would have applauded the skill of the republic's negotiators as they played off the various powers against each other, dipping into the city's bountiful gold reserves when all else failed. The word proudly emblazoned on their flag was *Libertas* (freedom).

Stradun, Dubrovnik

The sweeping Stradun, also known as the Placa, is Dubrovnik's main thoroughfare, cutting a pedestrianized swathe right through the Old City. Formed when the narrow channel that separated the Slavic settlement of Dubrovnik on the mainland from the Roman settlement on the island of Raus was filled in during the 12th century, it has survived the disastrous earthquake of 1667 and Serb shelling during the Siege of Dubrovnik from 1991 to 1992. Today this smooth limestone walkway, with its melée of attractive shops, cafés, bars and restaurants, buzzes with visitors throughout the summer months.

Sponza Palace

🔵 The Café Festival, housed in one of the Stradun's graceful stone houses, is the place to be and be seen on the Stradun. During the Dubrovnik Festival, you will have to be quick to snare one of the coveted outside tables.

🔵 Even if you have seen the Stradun by day, you should also return at night, when floodlighting gives the thoroughfare a more romantic ambience.

• Church of St Saviour: Map H4. Open 9am–4pm daily
• Franciscan Monastery: Map H4. Open 9am–6pm daily. Adm charge 15kn (children 7.50kn); discount for groups
• Church of St Blaise: Map J5. Open 8am–8pm daily. Free
• Museum to the Dubrovnik Defenders: Sponza Palace. 020 321 032. Map J5. Open 8am–2pm daily. Free

Top 10 Sights

1. Shutters and Lamps
2. Café Culture
3. Onofrio's Large Fountain
4. Church of St Saviour
5. Franciscan Monastery
6. Orlando's Column
7. Clocktower
8. Sponza Palace
9. Onofrio's Little Fountain
10. Church of St Blaise

1 Shutters and Lamps

For a wonderfully controlled piece of town planning, look at the window shutters and the lamps along the Stradun *(right)*. They are all painted the same shade of green, giving a cohesiveness not often found in European cities these days.

2 Café Culture

Join the locals for a drink and watch the world go by *(above)*. Many Stradun cafés fling tables out at the first flash of sunshine, but getting a seat can be an ordeal at the height of summer.

Stradun

3 Onofrio's Large Fountain

Damaged in the Siege of 1991–2, this 15th-century fountain *(below)* has been restored. Once, travellers would stop here to wash in its gushing waters.

Share your travel recommendations on traveldk.com

4 Church of St Saviour
The staid Renaissance façade does little to hint at the colour inside. Here regular concerts (above) and art exhibitions, often with work by modern Dalmatian artists, are held.

5 Franciscan Monastery
The dark cloisters and lush vegetation of this 14th-century monastery conjure up echoes of the Dubrovnik of old, as do the fascinating exhibits of the Monastery Museum. Arrive early to avoid the crowds (see pp12–13).

6 Orlando's Column
Mystery surrounds the statue (left) that guards the spot where the Stradun unfurls into Luža Square. Some locals claim that this legendary knight saved the city from disaster when he fought off menacing pirates in the 8th century.

7 Clocktower
A striking timepiece (right), this clocktower dates from the 15th century. Overhauled in 1929, the duo of bell strikers visible today are copies. The originals are in the Sponza Palace.

8 Sponza Palace
The inscription "We are forbidden to cheat and use false measures, and when I weigh goods, God weighs me", reveals this early-16th-century palace's former role as the city's customs house and mint. Today it is home to the State Archives and the Museum to the Dubrovnik Defenders.

9 Onofrio's Little Fountain
Tucked into a building by the Rector's Palace, this "little sister" to the large Onofrio fountain often goes unnoticed. It dates from the 15th century.

10 Church of St Blaise
This church (right) sits at the top of the Stradun. Inside, Dubrovnik's patron saint, St Blaise, cradles a model of the city showing what it looked like before the earthquake of 1667.

Earthquake of 1667
The earthquake of 1667 tore the heart out of Gothic and Renaissance Dubrovnik, killing 5,000 of its citizens and reducing many of its key buildings to rubble. This terrible tragedy paved the way for the construction of one of the most impressive Baroque cities in Europe. Carefully planned to sit within the protective confines of the sturdy city walls, it resisted all intruders until the arrival of Napoleonic troops in the early 19th century.

For Dubrovnik's best cafés See p65

Left **Romanesque cloisters** Middle **Church of St Francis** Right **Gothic portal**

Franciscan Monastery, Stradun

1 Romanesque Cloisters
Mihoje Brajkov's magnificent 14th-century cloisters, with their graceful, double-pillared columns deserve a close look. Visit in the early morning or late afternoon, before they become too crowded.

2 Inner Courtyard
Step into this inner sanctum to view the cloisters and admire the spectacular balustrade that frames the courtyard.

3 Frescoes
The life of St Francis and his animals is depicted in the frescoes that line the cloisters.

4 Belltower
The dome-topped belltower dominating the western end of the Stradun dates from the 14th century and features Gothic and Romanesque elements. Its majestic presence towers over the monastery courtyard.

5 Pharmacy
The monastery is home to one of the oldest pharmacies in Europe, with a collection of treatments and pharmacopoeias dating from the 15th century. The dispensary is still operational (8am–2pm, Mon–Sat).

6 Church of St Francis
Most of the original 14th-century church was destroyed by the Great Earthquake of 1667. Remarkable features in this 18th-century reconstruction include the lavish marble altars and the ornate organ framed by cherubs.

7 Gothic Portal
An imposing *Pietà* by Petar and Leonardo Petrovič crowns this southern portal, all that remains of the original 14th-century church.

8 Library
The monastery museum is home to Croatia's largest collection of historical manuscripts, over 1,200, dating from the early Middle Ages.

9 Portraits
The library walls are adorned with portraits of some of the city's most celebrated citizens, including the mathematician Ruđer Bošković (1711–87).

10 Ivan Gundulić Memorial
A plaque on the north wall of the church commemorates the 17th-century poet Ivan Gundulić, who is buried in the monastery.

Belltower

For visitor information for the Fransiscan Monastery and its museum **See p10**

Left **Dubrovnik Painting** Middle **Stone relief of St Francis** Right **Re-creation of the old pharmacy**

🔟 Franciscan Monastery Museum

1 Dubrovnik Painting
This painting is a revealing insight into how medieval Dubrovnik looked, before the devastating earthquake of 1667 felled the city.

2 Missile Damage
On 6 December 1991, known locally as "Black Tuesday", Serbian missiles reigned down on Dubrovnik. Two shell-holes have been left in the museum walls to serve as reminders of the damage sustained by the monastery.

Portrait of St Blaise

Missile damage

3 War Record
Inconspicuously located below the painting of Dubrovnik is a book cataloguing the devastation caused by the 54 direct hits upon the monastery during the siege of the city in 1991–2.

4 Missiles
Tucked into a corner, by a bench near the entrance to the museum, lie the casings of some of the missiles that wrought destruction on this tranquil space.

5 St Blaise's Foot
The most prized possession in the reliquary collection is this foot of St Blaise, preserved in a boot-like gold and silver case.

6 Religious Painting
The highlight of the museum's collection of religious art is a 15th-century portrait of St Blaise, set against a striking gold backdrop.

7 Osman
One of the treasures of the museum's library is an 18th-century transcript of Ivan Gundulić's *Osman*. Heralded as the poet's masterpiece, it celebrates a famous Slavic victory over the Turks.

8 Potions and Poisons
Set in a re-creation of the monastery's original pharmacy are row upon row of measuring instruments and traditional remedies, some lethal poisons.

9 Stone Reliefs
A small open space to one side of the museum contains odd remnants of carved masonry from the building, including gargoyles and segments of old gravestones.

10 St Francis
The medieval stone relief of St Francis, above the museum entrance, appears to be casting a protective eye over his domain.

🔟 Rector's Palace, Dubrovnik

The Rector of Dubrovnik wielded very little real power. Nominal head of the government, he was in office for a single month, during which he had to live away from his family and was only allowed to leave the palace on official business. The original building, more castle than palace, was blown up in 1435. The new building erected on the site had to be restored after another explosion in 1463, and again after the earthquake of 1667; today's palace is a hybrid of Gothic, Renaissance and Baroque styles. Dubrovnik no longer has a rector, but his opulent residence still plays an important role in the cultural life of the city.

Latin inscription at the top of the stairs

🔵 The recently renovated Gradska Kavana is a café fit for a Rector, with views across Luža Square and down the Stradun on one side and out onto the old port on the other.

🔵 The windows on the first floor make a perfect spot for photographing both the cathedral and the displays of folk dancing that sometimes take place in the street below. If you find the windows open, just pop out your lens and shoot.

- Pred Dvorom 3
- Map J5
- 020 321 422
- Open 9am–6pm daily
- Adm charge 35kn (children 15kn; groups 20kn)

Top 10 Sights

1. Gothic Loggia
2. Atrium
3. Statue of Miho Pracat
4. Gundulić Portrait
5. Statues of St Blaise
6. Prison Cells
7. Stairs
8. Inscription
9. Sedan Chairs
10. Rector's Study

Rector's Palace

Gothic Loggia
This ornately carved loggia *(above)* was built using marble from the Dalmatian island of Korčula. In the middle of the parade of Gothic columns and capitals are three in the Renaissance style.

Atrium
This compact open-air space offers a suitably grand welcome to visitors and, today, also serves as a venue for cultural events, such as recitals by the Dubrovnik Symphony Orchestra.

Statue of Miho Pracat
Taking pride of place in the atrium is Piero Paolo's 17th-century statue of shipping magnate Miho Pracat *(left)*, from the nearby island of Lopud. Dying without an heir, he left his all his wealth to the Republic of Ragusa.

Gundulić Portrait
This is one of the few portraits in existence of Dubrovnik's most celebrated poet, Ivan Gundulić (1588–1638).

Keep your eyes peeled for statues of St Blaise dotted around the Old City.

5 Statues of St Blaise

The sculptures of St Blaise in the museum here afford a rare chance to get up close to the city's patron saint. Most other renderings hang well above head height, or behind distant glass in his eponymous church *(see p38)*.

Entrance

Key

First Floor

Ground Floor

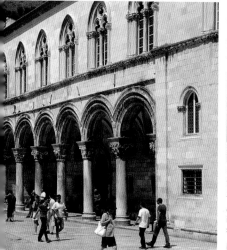

6 Prison Cells

The ground floor once served as the Republic of Ragusa's courtroom and prison. The dank, gloomy cells here hint at the harsh treatment meted out to inmates, who relied on friends and family for food and water.

7 Stairs

The rather ghoulish stairs up to the first floor are adorned with three lifelike hands on each rail. They were used only once a month, by the incoming rector at the start of his term of office.

An Explosive History

In addition to being the abode of the head of the Republic of Ragusa, as well as the site of the law courts and prison, the Rector's Palace also once served as a gunpowder store. This foolishness on the part of the authorities unfortunately resulted in the building being blown sky high on two occasions. It was only after the second disastrous explosion that the city's leaders finally made the decision to move their arsenal elsewhere.

8 Inscription

The inscription in Latin at the top of the stairs would have put any rector firmly in his place by reminding him of his duty to focus, not on his personal concerns, but only on public and civic matters.

9 Sedan Chairs

In the small room beneath the inscription is a collection of 18th-century sedan chairs *(right)*, that hints at the opulence of the city's nobility.

10 Rector's Study

In one of the Palace's most elegant and graceful rooms *(left)*, visitors can watch a rather lifeless looking dummy of the rector (in a garish red gown) hard at work on affairs of state.

🔟 Korčula Town

It's easy to see why the explorer Marco Polo would have been drawn back to his native town Korčula (assuming, that is, that it really was his native town, a matter of some debate). There is no doubting the beauty of the place, a mosaic of terracotta rooftops encircled by medieval walls and punctuated by church spires, jutting out into the cobalt blue of the Adriatic with the majestic Pelješac mountains as a backdrop. Evidence of former Venetian rule abounds, from the proud Venetian lions adorning its buildings to a cathedral dedicated to St Mark.

Cathedral of St Mark

🔊 Housed in an old bastion, the Massimo bar offers sweeping views out across the Pelješki Channel.

☞ In high season, visit on Mondays and Thursdays to enjoy the Moreška *(see opposite and p55).*

- Map H1
- Tourist Information: Obala Franje Tuđmana. 020 715 701
- Cathedral of St Mark: Trg Sv Marka Statuta. Open 9am–7pm daily (until 9pm in summer)
- Bishop's Palace: Trg Sv Marka Statuta. 020 711 049. Open Jun–Aug: 9am–7pm daily; Sep–May: by appt. Adm charge 15kn
- Civic Museum: Trg Sv Marka Statuta. 020 711 420. Open Jun–Sep: 9:30am–9pm Mon–Sat; Oct–May: 9:30am–2pm Mon–Sat. Adm charge 10kn (children 3kn)
- Marco Polo House: Depolo. Open Jul–Aug: 10am–1pm, 5–7pm, Mon–Sat. Adm charge 10kn

Top 10 Features

1. City Walls
2. Land Gate and Steps
3. Town Hall
4. Cathedral of St Mark
5. Bishop's Palace
6. Town Museum
7. Marco Polo House
8. Art Shops/Arneri Palace
9. Churches
10. Beaches

City Walls

Korčula's city walls proved sturdy enough to see off an onslaught by the Ottoman Turks in 1571. Today large chunks of the fortifications have been cleared to make way for a road, although sections of wall do remain, with cannons peering out over the Pelješki Channel *(above)*, and a sprinkling of bastions still stand guard.

Land Gate and Steps

The sweep of steps up to the Land Gate *(right)* provides a dramatic entrance to the old town. Set in a 14th-century bastion, the gate was once a crucial strongpoint on the walls.

Korčula Town

Town Hall

The 16th-century town hall sits just inside the Land Gate. Its small loggia recalls Korčula Town's Venetian heritage.

Cathedral of St Mark

This cathedral, completed in the 15th century, is one of the most charming ecclesiastical buildings in the Adriatic islands. The interior is a riot of Gothic and Renaissance styles.

Bishop's Palace

To the south of the cathedral stands the Bishop's Palace, with a statue of Mary, Queen of Scots. Artworks, including the cathedral treasury, are displayed here. The highlights of the collection are paintings by Bassano and Carpaccio *(right)*.

Town Museum

In the main square opposite the cathedral is a small civic museum, housed in the striking 16th-century Gabriellis Palace. Among a number of interesting exhibits here is a copy of a 4th-century Greek tablet.

Marco Polo House

Allegedly the great explorer's birthplace, this house is currently being restored and developed as a museum devoted to his life. The attached tower offers fine views of the rooftops of Korčula Town.

Churches

Korčula Town may be small, but it manages to cram in a wealth of churches. Look out for the All Saint's Church *(left)*, St Michael's and the Church of our Lady, which all stand within the old town walls.

Art Shops/Arneri Palace

Korčula Town overflows with small art shops that sell everything from standard depictions of the local skyline right through to more esoteric works of modern art. The art shop housed within the Arneri Palace, on the same square as the cathedral, is a good place to start.

Beaches

East of the town lie a series of small beaches that make pleasant spots to swim on hot days. A short bus-ride (or in season, boat-ride) away are better beaches at Lumbarda *(above)*.

Moreška

Korčula is the only Dalmatian island where real swords are still used for dancing the Moreška (literally, "Moorish"). Dating from the 12th century, the dance has been performed in Korčula since the 16th, and is believed to be a re-enactment of the victory of Christianity over Islam in Spain. Today's simplified form sees the White Knight (Christianity) fight the Black Knight (Islam), for the affections of a Muslim maiden. The White knight triumphs, and the maiden converts to Christianity.

🔟 Trogir

Trogir, listed as a UNESCO World Heritage Site, is quite simply one of the most stunning places in the Mediterranean. Sitting on its own island with bridges linking it to the mainland on one side and to the island of Čiovo on the other, the town forms a shimmering knot of orange roofs and traditional stone buildings, amongst which lies one of Croatia's most remarkable cathedrals. The well-preserved old centre is perhaps the most unified in the whole country, a pedestrianized oasis where the centuries peel back with every step. Even the heavy crowds in summer fail to diminish Trogir's appeal.

Land Gate

🌴 The palm-fringed Riva is ideal for a relaxed coffee or meal at any time.

✪ Cross the bridge to the island of Čiovo for great views across to the old city.

- Map D5
- Tourist Information: Trg Ivana Pavla II. 021 881 412
- Cathedral of St Lawrence Bell Tower: Trg Ivana Pavla II. 021 881 426. Open Jun–Sep: 9am–12pm, 4pm–7pm daily. Adm charge 10kn
- Kamerlengo Fortress. Open Jun–Sep: 9am–8pm daily. Adm charge 10kn
- Civic Museum: ulica Gradska Urata 4. 021 881 406. Open 9am–1pm, 5–9pm daily. Adm charge 15kn (children 5kn); discount for groups
- Church of St John the Baptist: Trg Ivana Pavla II. Closed for renovation until further notice
- Convent of St Nicholas: Gradska 2. Open May–Sep: 9am–12pm, 4pm–7pm daily; Oct–Apr: by appt. Adm charge 5kn

Top 10 Features

1. Cathedral of St Lawrence
2. Kamerlengo Fortress
3. Civic Museum
4. Loggia and Clock Tower
5. Čipiko Palace
6. Marmont's Gazebo
7. Church of St John the Baptist
8. Convent of St Nicholas
9. Riva
10. Land Gate

Cathedral of St Lawrence

Highlights include the 13th-century west door, lavishly adorned with biblical scenes carved by Trogir-born sculptor Radovan, and the sumptuous Renaissance styling of the baptistry and St John's Chapel *(above)*. The adjacent Zupni Dvor houses an interesting collection of 14th- to 17th-century paintings.

Kamerlengo Fortress

This fortification *(below)* has guarded the western approaches to Trogir since the 15th century. Concerts and film showings are held here in summer, while the ramparts offer views of the old town.

Riva

Civic Museum

Trogir's civic museum is housed in the Baroque Garagnin Palace and presents details of the town's eclectic past. It houses everything from the legacy left by the Greeks and Romans to chilling documents from the Napoleonic era, listing the proclamation of death sentences on local officials who dared to defy French authority.

Note that opening hours have a tendency to change, so it's best to check in advance if your time is limited.

Loggia and Clock Tower

Traditionally a place where criminals were tried and shamed, the 14th-century loggia *(left)* is notable for the conspicuous gap on its eastern wall, left when a Venetian stone lion was blown up by local activists in the 1930s, in a show of defiance against Italian claims on Dalmatian territory.

Čipiko Palace

This grand Gothic edifice *(below)* is one of the most impressive of the town's old palaces. It was once the base of the powerful Čipiko family, who held great influence in 15th-century Trogir.

Marmont's Gazebo

During the Napoleonic era (1806–13) the top French General in the region, Marmont, liked nothing better than to recline, here taking in the views and indulging in the odd game of cards. It is still a striking spot, despite the more recent Čiovo shipyards.

Church of St John the Baptist

This small Romanesque church, all that remains of a great Benedictine monastery, is the final resting-place of the Čipiko family. Here you can see their tomb, decorated with a 15th-century relief depicting *The Mourning of Christ*.

Convent of St Nicholas

This modest convent is worth visiting for its art collection. The highlight, only uncovered in the 1920s, is the 3rd-century Greek relief of Kairos *(left)*. Note too the chests used by new arrivals for bringing gifts into the convent.

Riva

The waterfront Riva is where locals and tourists come to wander or enjoy a meal or drink on balmy summer evenings. In season, boats line up here and visitors can book trips for the next day.

Land Gate

The most impressive surviving gate, this forms part of the fortifications built by the Venetians. A statue of St John, Trogir's patron saint, watches warily over new arrivals from the mainland.

Trogir Orientation

Vehicles are banned from Trogir's historic core. However, those arriving by car can park in the public car park located just outside the old town's northern walls; simply cross over the bridge from the mainland and turn right. Parking spaces are at a premium in summer, so many people opt to take the bus instead. The bus station is sited not far from the aforementioned bridge, on the Jadranska Magistrala.

Krka National Park

Krka National Park is one of southern Europe's scenic wonders, a green oasis in an otherwise parched landscape. Spread over 109 sq km (42 sq miles) to the north-east of Šibenik, it tracks the route of the Krka river, with its spectacular waterfalls, gurgling pools and pounding rapids. Swimming is possible in places, making the park the perfect place for a hot day, but it's well worth a visit whatever the weather. As well as the wildlife and picturesque historic buildings, there are plenty of idyllic spots just to sit and gaze at the glorious surroundings.

General view of Krka National Park

🖲 Near the boat landing at Roški, Slap, Kristijan, a small agritourism venture, offers homemade *pršut (see p49)*, cheese and bread, not to mention friendly owners with a penchant for dishing out lethal strength *rakija* (a fruit spirit).

🛈 Those who are looking to cover the park from Skradin right through to the Krka Monastery should arrive early and be prepared for a very long day.

- Map C3
- Park Office: Trg Ivana Pavla II, 22001 Šibenik. 022 217 720
- www.npkrka.hr
- Open summer: 8am–6pm; winter: 9am–5pm
- Adm charge 25–80kn, depending on season

Top 10 Features

1. Skradin
2. Lake Visovac
3. Mills and Exhibition
4. Skradinski Buk
5. Visovac Monastery
6. Medu Gredama Gorge
7. Roški Slap
8. Krka Monastery
9. Nečven Fortress
10. Wildlife

Skradin
Guarding the southern entrance to the park is this charming little waterfront town *(above)*, which is fast becoming a favourite with the sailing fraternity – the marina is open year-round. The sprinkling of decent seafood restaurants here makes it a good location for a relaxing meal after a long day's exploration in the park.

Skradinski Buk
Water thunders 47 m (154 ft) over the 17 steps that transport it down the hillside here into a large rock pool that makes a wonderful swimming venue. Views from the walkway ascending the hillside are breathtaking.

Visovac Monastery

Mills and Exhibitions
At Skradinski Buk and Roški Slap *(below)*, several disued mills have been turned into craft shops and galleries. Staff in period costume are on hand for photographs.

Lake Visovac
Just to the north of Skradinski Buk, the river opens out into this wide, reed-fringed expanse. In summer, fire-fighting planes may be seen here, swooping down for water to extinguish forest fires.

Visovac Monastery
Founded by Franciscans in the 14th century, this chocolate-box monastery reclining on an island in the middle of Lake Visovac makes a popular boat trip. Set in lush gardens, the monastery has a small church, a modest museum, and a gem of a library.

Među Gredama Gorge
The Krka river narrows into a steep-sided gorge between Lake Visovac and Roški Slap. Walls of sheer rock rise up like skyscrapers on both sides, to well over 100 m (328 ft) in places.

Krka National Park

Roški Slap
The best way to approach this swathe of roaring water *(above)*, as it plummets down into the gorge, is by boat. The longest drop of this waterfall is over 25 m (82 ft), as the river Krka forges a path through the dense vegetation of the surrounding forests.

Krka Monastery
This fine Orthodox monastery on the banks of the Krka (also known as St Archangel) lies at the northern end of the park – a two-hour boat excursion from the upper end of Roški Slap. Once there, you are rewarded by a memorable collection of icons, paintings, books and textiles.

Nečven Fortress
A 14th-century Croat stronghold, the Nečven Fortress *(above)* may be little more than a ruin, but it casts a haunting presence over the Krka as the river makes its way through the narrow gorge here.

Wildlife
Around a thousand different plant species have been recorded in the park *(left)*, as well as numerous species of bird, 18 species of bat and nine types of snake, including a venomous viper.

Krka National Park Orientation

The most dramatic way to reach the park is by boat from Skradin. From the landing pier, the entrance and Skradinski Buk are just a short walk to the south. Most visitors stick to the well-worn tourist path, but you can also follow a trail of wooden walkways and bridges along the cascade formations. Head up the hill, beyond the old mills and the visitor parking, where information boards detail the park's various boat tours; here you can buy tickets, and will be directed to the boats.

🔟 Diocletian's Palace, Split

Split's city centre is like no other in Europe. Built as a grand retirement home for the Roman Emperor Diocletian, its character was later modified by refugees from nearby Salona who fled there in 614, after their own city was sacked. It may be crumbling and ramshackle in parts, but the area occupied by the once mighty imperial palace – now a UNESCO World Heritage site – has about 3,000 residents and is crammed with busy bars and boutique art shops. Unlike much of the Dalmatian coast, the whole complex buzzes with life all year round and dishes up a varied choice of things to see and do.

The cathedral belltower, looming over the port

🍴 The spacious Luxor Café in the sunken square is a good place to relax and refuel.

🧭 Delve beyond the cupola to explore the upper tier of the palace. There are few major sights, but it is a lot quieter here and there are good views of the Adriatic as well as a couple of lively bars at night.

- Map P3
- Tourist information: Peristyle. 021 345 606
- Subterranean Chambers: Open 8am–6pm daily. Adm charge 10kn
- Cathedral of St Domnius: Peristyle. 021 342 589. Open 7am–noon, 4–7pm daily. Adm charge 10kn
- Belltower: Peristyle. Open 8am–7pm daily. Adm charge 10kn
- City Museum: Papalićeva 1. 021 344 917. Jun–Sep: 9am–9pm daily; Oct–May: 9am–4pm Tue–Fri, 10am–1pm Sat, Sun. Adm charge 15kn (children 5kn)

Top 10 Sights

1. Subterranean Chambers
2. Main Hall
3. Peristyle
4. Cathedral of St Domnius
5. Belltower
6. Baptistry
7. Cupola
8. City Museum
9. Golden Gate
10. Iron Gate

1 Subterranean Chambers

The palace's underground vaults mirror the layout of the floor above. Now open as a museum, they give a good impression of the palace's former appearance.

2 Main Hall

The main subterranean hall of the palace houses an alley of souvenir shops. Here you can buy anything from postcards to paintings and statues of Roman figures.

3 Peristyle

Once an antechamber to Diocletian's quarters, the dramatic, colonnaded square known as the Peristyle *(above)* is the heart of the palace complex.

Main Hall, Diocletian's Palace

4 Cathedral of St Domnius

Built over Diocletian's tomb, the main structure here is Roman. Inside is a 13th-century pulpit *(below)* and work by 15th-century sculptor Juraj Dalmatinac.

➡ *"Peristyle" is the name given to a colonnade surrounding a courtyard – also to the courtyard itself.*

Belltower

The belltower, which soars high above the cathedral, was not completed until the early 20th century. The panoramic views of the city that it offers *(above)* make the long climb up to the top well worth the effort.

Bronze Gate

Baptistry

An alley opposite the cathedral leads to the Bapistry, once the Roman Temple of Jupiter. Inside, a striking feature is the sculpture of John the Baptist *(below)* by Ivan Meštrović (1883–1962).

Cupola

Stone steps from the sunken square lead to a domed area, where guests once waited for an audience with the Emperor. At night, stars are visible through a gap in the top of the dome.

Golden Gate

This sturdy portal once led north to the nearby settlement of Salona. Today, it is being restored to its full splendour, thanks to funding by a local bank.

City Museum

East of the sunken square, the City Museum is housed in the 15th-century Papalič Palace. Among the artifacts relating to Split's history is a collection of weaponry and armour *(left)*.

Iron Gate

Split's most striking gate has its own church (Our Lady of the Belfry) and clock tower. A café on Narodni Trg will make an ideal spot from which to admire this elegant portal.

Diocletian's Palace Orientation

From the waterfront Riva, Diocletian's Palace can be entered through the Bronze Gate. Head north through the main hall and go up the steps at the far end into the Peristyle, with its elegant colonnades and imposing cathedral. Just north of the cathedral is the city's most centrally located tourist office – a great place to pick up visitor information and maps. From the Peristyle, the main sights are easy to find – just a couple of minutes walk to north, east, west or south.

Leave the palace by the Golden Gate to see Ivan Meštrović's imposing statue of Grgur of Nin (see p41).

Left **Riva** Right **View from Marjan Hill**

🔟 Other Sights in Split

1 Riva
Split's palm-fringed, pedestrianized waterfront is where its citizens come to meet up and be seen. The many pavement cafés make this the perfect spot to relax and gaze seawards at the ferries, as they slip off to the nearby islands. ✆ *Map N2*

2 Meštrović Gallery
The Croatian-born, Expressionist sculptor Ivan Meštrović (1883–1962) may not have realized his dream of retiring to this bolthole in Split, but it now provides a fitting home for a fine collection of his work *(see p40)*.

3 Marjan Hill
From the west side of the town, steps lead up to this stretch of greenery, part of a protected nature reserve. The views from the top are spectacular, with the mountains stretching off towards Bosnia in the distance and large swathes of the Dalmatian coast and its many islands visible on a clear day. ✆ *Map N5*

4 Archeological Museum
The collections housed here feature a wide variety of artifacts that date from the Roman, early Christian and medieval periods in Split, as well as a smaller legacy from the time of Greek rule in Dalmatia *(see p40)*.

5 Marmontova
This elegant and modern street on the western edge of Diocletian's Palace is awash with designer shops. In the late afternoon, it attracts throngs of smartly attired, window-shopping locals. ✆ *Map N2*

Distant Agreements, ✆ *Map N2*
Meštrović Gallery

6 Fish Market
This wonderfully pungent and colourful market bursts into life every morning (except on Sunday, when it is closed). Here you can feast your eyes on the rich spread of Adriatic seafood, accompanied by a cacophony of gesticulating sellers and hollering locals.

7 Narodni Trg
When the Venetians rumbled into Split, they moved the focus of the city away from Diocletian's Palace, westwards and into this square. Highlights here are the 15th-century town hall and its grandiose ground-floor loggia. ✆ *Map P2*

Fish Market

8 Trg Republike

In contrast to the Roman and Venetian parts of town, this square's grand architecture hints at old Vienna. ◈ Map N2

9 Bačvice

A short walk southeast from the centre of Split leads to this small bay, with one of the city's most popular summer beaches, a large waterfront entertainment centre and a buzzing nightlife (see p86). ◈ Map Q6

10 Coastal Walk

The coastline stretching out from Bačvice is lined with beaches, cafés and nightclubs. Wimbledon champion Goran Ivanišević launched his career at a tennis club near here. ◈ Map Q6

Top 10 Events in Diocletian's Life

1. AD 245: Born into a lowly Dalmatian family in Salona
2. 282: Finds favour with Emperor Carus, and is made a Roman Count
3. 283: Carus elevates his status to that of consul
4. 284: Reaches his zenith, at the age of just 39, by becoming Roman Emperor
5. 295: Commissions his seaside retirement palace in Split, which takes around a decade to complete
6. 303: Outlaws Christianity, ordering the destruction of all churches and the persecution of Christians
7. 305: Becomes the first Roman emperor to retire rather than die or be murdered in the job
8. 308: Declines request to be reinstated as emperor
9. 315: Diocletian's wife (Prisca) and daughter (Valeria) are murdered by Emperor Licinius
10. c.316: Poisons himself in his palace at Split

Emperor Diocletian

The life of Diocletian is a true "rags to riches" story. He grew up in a family of modest means in the Dalmatian town of Salona, before embarking on a meteoric rise through the military ranks of the Roman Empire to assume the top position. He demonstrated a marked taste for grand construction projects; his greatest legacy to Croatia is the lavish retirement palace he built by the Adriatic, later to evolve into the city of Split. Retirement was an unconventional move for a Roman emperor – one way or another, all of his predecessors had died in the job. From his grand seaside residence, Diocletian looked on as the Empire began to crumble, and it was here that he eventually took his own life. Given Diocletian's notoriety as a persecutor of Christians, it is ironic that Split's cathedral was later built on the site of his tomb.

Diocletian condemning St Cosmas and St Damian (predella from the Annalena Altarpiece by Fra Angelico, 1434)

🔟 Kornati National Park

Perhaps the writer George Bernard Shaw summed it up best when he gushed "On the last day of the Creation, God desired to crown his work, and thus created the Kornati Islands ..." There is nothing in Europe quite like this necklace of 89 starkly beautiful islands, gleaming white against the deep blue of the Adriatic. Designated a national park in 1980, they are sparsely populated, as few people have been successful in eking out any kind of living on these rocky strips of land. Today, the Kornati Islands are popular with day-trippers, sailors and stressed-out city dwellers looking to get away from it all.

Typical island of white rock, bare of vegetation

🛒 The grocery store near ACI Piškera marina on the Panitula Vela islet is one of the few places where you can buy food and drinks out of season.

🌀 The islands' sheltered waters are perfect for novice sailors.

- Map B4
- Kornati National Park Office: Butina 2, 22243 Murter. 022 435 740. www.kornati.hr. Adm charge 40/80kn (purchased inside/outside park)
- In season, tickets can be bought at marinas in Betina (Dugi Otok), Murter, Biograd Na Moru, Zadar and Punat. The National Park Office in Muter sells tickets year round.
- Murter-based travel agencies arranging island accommodation include Coronata (www. coronata.hr), Kornat Turist (www.kornatturist.hr) and Žut Tours (www. zuttours.hr)

Top 10 Features

1. Murter
2. Sailing
3. Island Getaways
4. Kornat
5. Seafood Restaurants
6. Katina
7. Piškera
8. Lavsa
9. Mana
10. Wildlife

The steep cliffs of Mana

Murter

Murter harbour *(above)* is the main starting point on the mainland for trips into the National Park. Many ex-islanders (the Kornatari), whose families bought land on the islands for grazing their livestock during the 19th century, have now settled in Murter.

Sailing

A variety of companies, both Croatian and foreign, run day trips from Murter, Zadar, Šibenik and even Trogir to the Kornatis *(right)*. They can also organize a week's sailing, either bareback (without a skipper) or as a charter (with a skipper, who will also do the cooking).

Island Getaways

Visitors can live like Robinson Crusoe by hiring their own private island. Without any electricity or running water, their only human contact will be the supply boat that drops by every few days.

Kornat

The largest island in the National Park, Kornat *(above)*, is just 25 km (16 miles) long and 2.5 km (2 miles) wide. Sprinkled among its old stone houses are a few decent restaurants, a 6th-century Byzantine lookout tower and a small church.

Seafood Restaurants

In summer, a number of enterprising locals turn their old stone houses, many of which have small jetties, into restaurants. They offer first-rate, fresh, simply presented seafood to passing sailors.

Katina

At the northern tip of this island, the Mala Proversa waterway separates the Kornatis from Dugi Otok on the mainland. In the middle of this channel lie the remains of an ancient villa, dating back to a time when the islands were a fashionable holiday resort for wealthy Romans.

Piškera

Another island with a discernible Roman legacy is Piškera. There was once a substantial village here, though all that remains these days is the ruined shell of this settlement and an old church. The marina on Piškera *(right)* is the most developed in the islands.

Lavsa

Its good choice of sheltered, sandy coves make Lavsa a popular destination with the yachting fraternity. There they can stop off and idle away an afternoon, swimming and basking in the sunshine.

Mana

Mana is best known for three things: its flora, its ruined village – not in fact a real settlement but a set built for the 1950s film *The Cruel Sea* – and its steep, overhanging cliffs, a spectacular sight when the Adriatic swell crashes against them.

Wildlife

Attempts at exploiting the limited natural resources of the islands may appear to have stripped them of all wildlife. Yet they are home to over 300 plant varieties and a similar number of animal species, including wild sheep *(below)*.

Kornati Islands Orientation

The Kornati Islands National Park is located approximately seven nautical miles west of Murter and around 15 nautical miles from Zadar and Šibenik. In the summer, boats authorized to take tourists into the park line the waterfronts of these three towns. If you are thinking of booking a day trip, ask to see a map first to ensure that the tour really does include the park. The best way, however, to explore the park's many islands thoroughly is on a private yacht.

For more about sailing in Dalmatia **See pp46–7**

🔟 Cathedral of St James, Šibenik

For over a century, the citizens of Šibenik struggled to finance the building of one of the Mediterranean's largest and finest cathedrals. Now, this remarkably harmonious blend of Gothic and Renaissance styling dominates the city. When the main architect, Juraj Dalmatinac, died in 1475, his pupil Nikola Firentinac took over, completing the presbytery, choir, galleries, vaulted roof and dome. It has taken international experts several years to restore the building since its damage by Serbian shelling in 1991, during Croatia's war of independence. It was declared a UNESCO World Heritage Site in 2001.

A face carved on the cornice of the apse

○ The Gradska Vječnica café, opposite the cathedral, makes a good spot to sit and admire the splendours of this great building, over coffee or perhaps a leisurely lunch.

○ To appreciate the visual impact of the cathedral better, climb up to the nearby fortress of St Ana, from where you will be able to take in fully its massive scale as well as the grandeur of its exterior.

- Map C4
- Trg Republike Hrvatske 1
- Open May–Sep: 8:30am–noon, 6–8pm daily; Oct–Apr: 8:30am–noon, 4–6:30pm daily

Top 10 Features

1. Array of Heads
2. Façade
3. Door of Lions
4. Gothic Portal
5. Dome
6. Vaulted Roof
7. Interior
8. Transept
9. Presbytery
10. Baptistry

Array of Heads

These 72 stone heads adorn the exterior of the apse. They are reputed to represent, depending on whom you believe, either the cathedral's generous benefactors or locals who were too mean to dispense any of their wealth on the building's construction.

Inside Šibenik Cathedral

Door of Lions

Two stone lions guard Juraj Dalmatinac's finely crafted portico, supporting statues of Adam and Eve *(below)*. The doorway itself is framed by ornately carved spiral columns.

Façade

Taking 105 years to complete (1431–1536), the cathedral's symmetrical façade *(above)* is crafted from local limestone and Brač marble. Its impressive dimensions are 38 m (125 ft) by 14 m (46 ft). Look out for the angel standing protectively above the north portal.

4 Gothic Portal
The sculptures of various saints sweep around the arch of the main west door, although many of these figures have lost a limb or been decapitated down the years. Constructed during the first phase of building (1433–41), this elegant portal is one of the oldest parts of the cathedral.

5 Dome
Nikola Firentinac's cupola *(right)*, built around an octagonal drum, is guarded by statues of St Michael, St Martin and St James. Parts of today's structure are recent reconstructions, the original sustaining damage from Serb shells in the 1990s.

6 Vaulted Roof
Like the rest of the building, the roof was constructed using blocks of carefully measured stone, the individual pieces slotting together perfectly. It is widely regarded as a tribute to the great technical skill of the stonecutters involved.

7 Interior
This triple-aisled space is divided up by columns, topped by pointed arches. Notable features include the four massive pillars supporting the cupola, the tombs of Šibenik's bishops and the altars of the Three Kings and the Holy Cross.

9 Presbytery
Both architects – Dalmatinac and Firentinac – contributed to the presbytery's finely carved stone stalls *(above)*. Over them are further highly detailed, sculpted reliefs.

10 Baptistry
The small bapistry, at the end of the right aisle, houses a fine baptismal font supported by three putti *(right)*. A quartet of stone scallop shells leads up to the carved roof.

8 Transept
You may feel less than comfortable about walking under the transept after you learn that it was laced together without using mortar. Again, this is a testimony to the talent and prowess of the local stonemasons.

Šibenik Cathedral Orientation
Šibenik's cathedral is at the heart of the old town, which tumbles downhill from the main street, Kralja Zvonimira, to the north, toward the Adriatic, to the south. It is an easy walk west along the waterfront from the bus station or a short taxi ride from the train station. There is limited car parking on Obala Franje Tuđmana, the waterfront street just south of the city walls; from Kralja Zvonimira turn onto Vladimira Nazora, then take the third street on the right.

For more Dalmatian places of worship **See pp38–9**

🔟 Zadar Old Town

Despite being pummelled by Allied bombs during World War II and by Serb shells from 1991 to 1995, Zadar's old town boasts a wealth of attractions, all set within a pedestrianized peninsula that overlooks the warm, azure waters of the Adriatic. In this lively city of just over 100,000 inhabitants are two cathedrals – one Catholic and one Orthodox – and the remains of a Roman forum, all squeezed into a compact historic centre that is awash with cafés, bars and good restaurants. Zadar has yet to be "discovered" by mass tourism, but in summer its streets buzz with visitors from other parts of Croatia.

Amphorae in the Archeological Museum

🍺 Stop off at the Forum Café and sip a cold *pivo* (beer) or *bijela kava* (milky coffee) at one of the outside tables that overlook the Roman Forum.

🚶 Stroll along the Obala Kralja Petra Krešmira IV in the evening to enjoy the full glory of Zadar's magnificent sunsets.

• Map B3
• Church of St Simeon: Trg Petra Zoranića 7. 023 316 166. Open Jun–Sep: 8am–noon, 6–8pm daily; Oct–May: open for mass
• Cathedral of St Anastasia: Trg Svete Stos. 023 251 708. Open 8am–1pm, 5–6:30pm daily
• Archeological Museum: Trg Opatice Čike 1. 023 250 542. Open Jun–Sep: 9am–1pm, 5–9pm Mon–Sat; Oct–May: 9am–2pm Mon–Sat. Adm charge 10kn
• Church of St Donat: winter: 9am–3pm daily; summer: 9am–11pm daily. Adm charge 10kn

Top 10 Features

1. Land Gate
2. Church of St Simeon
3. Five Wells Square
4. Narodni Trg
5. Široka
6. Roman Forum
7. Archeological Museum
8. Church of St Donat
9. Cathedral of St Anastasia
10. Church of St Elijah

Church of St Elijah, altar

1 Land Gate

This voluminous gate – thought to have been completed in the 16th century by Italian architect Michele Sanmicheli – guards the southern entrance to the old town. A Venetian lion *(above)* stares down from this portal, revealing Zadar's links with Venice.

2 Church of St Simeon

The church that stands here today is a 17th-century reconstruction. It is home to a 14th-century silver sarcophagus *(right)* that holds the remains of St Simeon. On his saint's day, 8 October, his relics are paraded around the city.

3 Five Wells Square

Late into the 19th century, this complex of wells was where the citizens of Zadar drew their fresh water. Each of the five wells is identical in design. Also on the square is the Captain's House, which has recently been renovated and hosts modern art exhibitions.

4 Narodni Trg

This busy square *(above)*, once the centre of Venetian Zadar, boasts a brace of pavement cafés and a Venetian-style town hall with a loggia and a 16th-century guard house. During the summer, there is often an arts and crafts market here.

Zadar Old Town

5 Široka

Due to bombing during World War II, this main artery through the old town features more than its fair share of bland, 1950s concrete buildings. But it also has chic cafés and shops that teem with life in the evening and at weekends.

6 Roman Forum

Little of this ancient forum remains, as many of its stones were used as building blocks for the rest of the old town. A pillar, where criminals were once flogged, still stands, along with a scattering of odd pieces of carved stonework.

7 Archeological Museum

Sited on the Roman Forum, the collections here feature various finds from the city and surrounding area, which document a swathe of Zadar's heritage from the Stone Age right through to the 11th century.

8 Church of St Donat

Also on the Roman Forum, this 9th-century church *(right)* is Croatia's largest Byzantine building. The unusual circular design gives it great acoustics for the summer concerts that are held here.

9 Cathedral of St Anastasia

Just north of St Donat's is this Romanesque cathedral, founded in the 9th century. The present structure dates from the 12th–13th centuries. The belltower was completed as late as 1893.

10 Church of St Elijah

Orthodox since the 18th century, this modest church stands in the small Serb enclave of the old town; itself worth a wander around. The collection of 16th–19th-century icons held here is impressive.

The Siege of Zadar

As war engulfed the fledgling Croatian Republic in August 1991, Yugoslav Army forces and Serb irregulars descended on Zadar, which lay perilously close to the disputed Krajina region, where Serbs had declared autonomy. They quickly captured the outskirts and the city's airport, but hastily marshalled Croat forces managed to avert the fall of the city. A brutal siege ensued, and it took the UN three months to broker a ceasefire. Even so, the shelling of Zadar continued until hostilities finally ceased in 1995.

Left **The siege of Dubrovnik, 1991** Right **Crusaders conquering Zadar, 1202**

🔟 Moments in Croatian History

1 4th Century BC: Greeks and Illyrians in Dalmatia
Greek settlers began to cross the seas and join the Illyrian tribes who had already been eking out a living on the Dalmatian coastline. As the population along the coastal strip expanded, trade links and proto-settlements started to flourish.

2 1st Century AD: Romans Move into Dalmatia
The Roman Empire surged eastwards, engulfing whole swathes of Croatia and snuffing out most of the indigenous opposition in the process. Wine production flourished as the conquerors brought their expertise to a land whose soil and climate made it perfect for producing both red and white wines.

3 6th Century AD: Arrival of Slavic Tribes
Slavic tribes from the north began to arrive on the Dalmatian coast.

4 AD925: First Croatian King Crowned
Croatia became a nation under King Tomislav, the "Father of the Croats", whose achievement it was to unite the country for the first time. Croatia's independence, however, was soon

quashed by the superior power of the Huns and the mighty Venetian doges. The latter soon started to wield greater influence over Dalmatia.

5 1202: City of Zadar Sacked by the Crusaders
The Dalmatian city of Zadar was attacked and looted by Christian Crusaders as the Balkans became a battleground for Christian Europe to the west and the increasingly powerful Ottoman Empire to the east. The Turkish threat was to grow over the following centuries.

6 1593: Battle of Sisak
In 1578, the Austrian Habsburgs had created the Vojna Krajina, a "military frontier" intended to prevent further Turkish advances into Europe. The decisive victory came at the landmark Battle of Sisak, just south of Zagreb, where the Ottomans were finally halted. Habsburg influence on Croatia continued right up until World War I.

7 1699: Dalmatia Under Venetian Control
Large swathes of Dalmatia fell under the control of Venice, although the Republic of Ragusa (Dubrovnik, *see pp8–9*) retained its independence from both Venice and Constantinople.

King Tomislav

Preceding pages **View of Dubrovnik's Old City from the south**

8 1808: Napoleon Annexes Republic of Ragusa

In 1806, French troops saved Dubrovnik from a month-long siege by Russian and Montenegrin forces. Two years later, Napoleon claimed Ragusa for France.

Napoleon Bonaparte

9 1945: Tito Comes to Power

The Croatian-born marshal came to power in the aftermath of World War II, and set about establishing a socialist republic where ethnic differences between Serbs, Croats, Macedonians, Slovenes, Montenegrins and Bosnians were suppressed in favour of allegiance to the "mother country". Until his death in 1980, Tito skilfully played the West off against the Soviet Bloc, and built one of the biggest armed forces in Europe.

10 1991: Croatia Declares its Independence

A landslide referendum saw Croatia declare independence from Yugoslavia. Irregular Serbian units, backed up by the Yugoslav military, attacked the fledgling republic and besieged Dubrovnik. Hostilities had ceased by the end of 1995, and all captured Croatian territory was returned by 1998.

Top 10 Historical Figures

1 Emperor Diocletian

Diocletian (245–316) chose to build his retirement palace on the Adriatic coast, founding Split in the process (see p25).

2 King Tomislav

Many Croats still consider Croatia's first king a hero.

3 Grgur of Nin

This 10th-century bishop campaigned for the use of the Croatian language (rather than Latin) in church services.

4 Napoleon Bonaparte

An unlikely champion of Slavic expression, Napoleon (1769–1821) promoted Slavic languages in schools in the Illyrian Provinces.

5 Ban Josip Jelačić

Croatian army officer and nationalist Jelačić (1801–59) stood up to the mighty Austro-Hungarian Empire.

6 Juraj Strossmayer

Bishop Strossmayer (1815–1905) called for a pan-Slavic state, helping to clear the way for the formation of Yugoslavia.

7 Ante Pavelić

Leader of the fascist Ustaše movement, Pavelić (1889–1959) became head of the short-lived Independent State of Croatia during World War II.

8 Marshal Tito

Tito (1892–1980) fought the Axis forces before leading Yugoslavia after World War II.

9 Franjo Tuđman

Tuđman (1922–99) became first president of the newly independent Croatia in 1991.

10 Stjepan Mesić

A former Tuđman ally, the current Croatian president (b. 1934) has reinvented himself as the respectable face of modern Croatian politics.

Left **Dubrovnik** Middle **Church of Our Lady of Spilica, Kut** Right **St Mark's Tower, Trogir**

Old Towns

1 Dubrovnik

Lord Byron's "Pearl of the Adriatic" is Croatia's most famous set-piece. Encapsulated within the hulking medieval walls is a perfectly preserved Baroque city-state, sandwiched between a sweep of limestone mountains to the north and the Adriatic to the south. Rediscovered by tourists in recent years, the Old City can get crowded in summer, but there's no disguising its allure *(see pp8–15, 58–66)*.

2 Korčula Town

This mini-Dubrovnik matches its more illustrious sibling in everything but scale. Enjoying its own rocky promontory, this old town, carved over the centuries by the Venetians, still feels like an oasis not yet well acquainted with the 20th century, let alone the 21st. Within its walls lie churches, seafood restaurants, and the site where, locals believe, their most famous son, Marco Polo, was born *(see pp16–17, 92)*.

3 Trogir

Set picturesquely on an islet between the mainland and the island of Čiovo, this grand creation can make a credible claim for the title of finest old town on the Adriatic coast. Trogir's unity of design makes it special, which is why the locals call it the "town museum" *(see pp18–19)*.

Church of Chrysogonus, Zadar

Split – old and new towns

4 Split

No staid museum piece, Split's old town is a living and breathing slice of history, formed around the confines of the Emperor Diocletian's palatial waterfront retirement home, and adapted over the centuries by the Splicani *(see pp22–3, 25)*.

5 Zadar

Neither World War II nor the bombing of the early 1990s could dent the spirit of this lively, bustling town. It may lack the architectural cohesion of Trogir, Korčula and Dubrovnik, but its stunning setting – reclining on its own peninsula in a flurry of churches, Roman ruins and pavement cafés – more than makes up for it *(see pp30–31)*.

6 Hvar Town

It is easy to see why Hvar Town is the summer getaway of choice for Croatia's cognoscenti. The charming old core, crammed with Venetian architecture, sweeps around a wide Adriatic bay. High up

Šibenik

above, a rambling fort watches over the summer scene of pavement cafés, fish restaurants and bobbing tour boats. The main square is dominated by the imposing contours of St Stephen's Cathedral *(see pp39, 84)*.

Kut (Vis Town)

Relatively few visitors have discovered the historic Kut district of Vis Town, with its outstanding Renaissance triple-naved church, Our Lady of Spilica, its swathe of old Venetian merchant dwellings, and its trio of first-rate restaurants. In the ramble of narrow lanes near the waterfront, old women hang out their washing from balconies built by wealthy Venetians, while the local cats look on *(see p84)*.

Šibenik

The most "Croatian" city on the coast (in that it wasn't built by the Romans or the Venetians), Šibenik boasts a charming old town that rambles up in search of the city's fort through a tangle of narrow streets that have not yet been airbrushed for the needs of mass tourism. The Cathedral of St James, over a hundred years in the making, is its glorious centrepiece *(see pp28–9, 73)*.

Pag Town

Pag's compact old town is largely the work of Dalmatian architect Juraj Dalmatinac, who expertly crafted a web of streets designed to afford inhabitants protection against the biting bora winds from the north. On one flank the Adriatic laps, while on the other three the starched white rocks of Pag island stretch away towards the hulking shadow of the distant Velebit Mountains *(see p77)*.

Lastovo Town

Unusually, Lastovo Town turns its back on the Adriatic and tumbles in the opposite direction. Architecturally less ornate than many other Dalmatian towns, its most striking buildings are a group of 20 or so Renaissance stone houses, characterized by their high, broad terraces *(see p95)*.

Left **Cathedral of St Stephen, Hvar** Middle **Cathedral of St James, Šibenik** Right **St Donat's, Zadar**

Cathedrals and Churches

1 Cathedral of St James, Šibenik

Dominating Šibenik, this UNESCO-World-Heritage-listed edifice is a blaze of Gothic and Renaissance styles. Its construction took more than a century and nearly bankrupted the town's citizens. The main architect, Dalmatian Juraj Dalmatinac, didn't live to see the finished creation; the work was completed by one of his own pupils, the very capable Nikola Firentinac (see pp28–9).

2 Cathedral of St Lawrence, Trogir

The 13th-century west portal by local master Radovan is the *pièce de resistance* of this remarkable cathedral. Look out for the figures of Adam and Eve on either side, standing proudly over a pair of Venetian lions (indicating the influence Venice once had over Trogir). Arranged around the upper sections of the portal are depictions of the saints, and calendar scenes of local life (see pp18–19).

3 Church of the Holy Cross, Nin

Spiritually and symbolically one of the most important churches in Croatia, the Church of the Holy Cross is also one of the oldest – it dates back to the 9th century, when the early Croatian kings were on the throne and Nin was the focal point of the country's religious life. What it lacks in size, it more than makes up for with its perfect proportions and unusual cylindrical design. ◈ Map B3

4 Church of St Nicholas, Nin

A short drive south of Nin brings you to one of the most charming ecclesiastical structures in Europe – a small, 11th-century church built on a former burial mound. Today it makes an intensely atmospheric sight, standing firm on a windswept plain with the Adriatic to one side and the stark, haunting expanse of the Velebit mountains rising up on the other. ◈ Map B3

5 Church of St Blaise, Dubrovnik

Dubrovnik's highly revered patron saint, St Blaise, is said to have saved the city from sacking at the hands of the Venetians. He

Church of St Blaise, Dubrovnik

In Dalmatia, admission to church buildings is generally free, unless there is a special exhibition or event on.

pops up throughout the city, but nowhere is he more pleasingly represented than in this 18th-century church dedicated to him *(see pp11, 59)*.

Dubrovnik Cathedral

Legend has it that Dubrovnik Cathedral was founded by Richard the Lionheart in gratitude for his life being spared during a violent storm that washed him up on the island of Lokrum. True or not, this is one of the country's most striking religious buildings. Among its treasures are impressive Baroque frescoes, the Byzantine skull case of St Blaise, and a fine *Ascension* by Titian *(see p59)*.

Cathedral of St Stephen, Hvar Town, Hvar

Be sure to pop in here if you are lucky enough to catch the door ajar – the opening hours are erratic and limited. The 16th-century Renaissance building stands on the site of an old Benedictine monastery. One highlight is the understated 13th-century *Madonna and Child* on the altar. ◈ *Map D6*

Church of St Michael, Komiža, Vis

The Church of St Michael sits amidst vines on a steep bluff overlooking the sleepy fishing town of Komiža. Ask locally for opening times. ◈ *Map D6*

Cathedral of St Anastasia, Zadar

Zadar's magnificent Romanesque cathedral, built from the 12th to 13th centuries, stands on the site of an earlier (9th-century)

Cathedral of St Anastasia, Zadar

Byzantine structure, which in turn had stood on the site of the Forum of the ancient Roman town of Jadar. Somewhat overshadowed by its rather more celebrated neighbour St Donat's, this survivor of Allied air raids and Serb shelling should not be overlooked. There is a plaque commemorating the visit of Pope Alexander in 1177 *(see p31)*.

Church of St Donat, Zadar

Last used as a church in 1797, this fine example of Byzantine architecture has become the emblem of Zadar. Like the cathedral nearby, it stands on the site of the old Roman forum. Latin inscriptions can be seen in both the interior and exterior stonework, as stones from the forum were used as building blocks *(see p31)*.

Left **Maritime Museum, Dubrovnik** Right **Archaeological Museum, Split**

Museums and Galleries

Distant Agreements, Meštrović Gallery, Split

1 Meštrović Gallery, Split

More than 80 of Ivan Meštrović's sculptures, including a huge *Pietà* and outdoor bronze works, can today be viewed at his former home. The dining room has been left largely as it was and contains the sculptor's furniture and family portraits. ◈ *Šetalište Ivana Meštrovića 46 • Map N6 • 021 340 800 • Open mid-May–Sep: 9am–9pm Tue–Sun; Oct–mid-May: 9am–4pm Tue–Sat, 10am–3pm Sun • Adm charge*

2 Museum of Croatian Archeological Monuments, Split

One of Croatia's oldest museums has a fine collection of jewellery, weapons, stonework and epigraphics (inscriptions carved on stone). ◈ *Šetalište Ivana Meštrovića 18 • Map N6 • 021 323 901 • www.mhas-split.hr • Open 9:30am–4pm, Tue–Fri, 9:30am–1pm Sat • Adm charge*

Carving, Museum of Croatian Archaeological Monuments

3 Archeological Museum, Split

Star exhibits at this museum include Ancient Greek ceramics, weaponry from the 6th to 9th centuries, over 70,000 coins, and amphorae recovered from shipwrecks. ◈ *Zrinjsko-Frankopanska 25 • Map P5 • 021 318 721 • Open Jun–Sep: 9am–1pm, 5–8pm Tue–Fri, 9am–1pm Sat & Sun; Oct–May: 9am–2pm Tue–Fri, 9am–1pm Sat & Sun • Adm charge*

4 Maritime Museum, Dubrovnik

The most interesting part of the collection illustrates Dubrovnik's naval might between the 12th and 14th centuries, when it threatened Venice's supremacy *(see p9)*.

5 Tusculum, Solin

This museum, based at the Roman ruins of Salona *(see p81)*, disseminates information about the site and organizes guided tours by prior arrangement. ◈ *Put Manastirina bb • Map D5 • 021 212 900 • Open summer: 7am–8pm Mon–Sat, 9am–2pm Sun; winter: 7am–3pm Mon–Sat, 8am–4pm Sun • Adm charge*

6 Museum of the Island of Brač, Škrip

Treasures from all over Brač are housed in the Radojković Tower, which shows traces of Illyrian, Roman and early Croatian architecture. ◈ *Map E5 • 021 630 033 • Open 10am–6pm daily (ask locally for key holder) • Adm charge*

Note that opening times are liable to change; it's advisable to check in advance of your visit.

7 Hermitage of Blaca, Brač

This 16th-century monastery and its contents, including correspondence between the last priest and the Royal Astronomical Society in London, have been frozen in time since 1963. Roaming goats and a stunning location enhance its appeal. Access on foot only. ◎ Map E5

Amphorae, Archaeological Museum, Vis Town

8 Archeological Museum, Vis Town

Sculptures, ceramics, weapons and everyday items illuminate life in the Ancient Greek town of Issa (modern Vis Town). ◎ Šetalis Viški boj 12 • Map D6 • 021 711 729 • Open summer: 9am–1pm, 5–7pm Tue–Sun; winter: 9am–1pm Tue–Sun • Adm charge

9 National Museum, Zadar

Housed in the Benedictine monastery, this museum documents Zadar and its environs from the 16th to the 19th centuries through photographs, paintings and impressive scale models. ◎ Poljana Pape Aleksandra III bb • Map B3 • 023 231 851 • Open 9am–noon, 5–8pm Mon–Fri; 9am–noon Sun • Adm charge

10 Archeological Museum, Zadar

The exhibits chart the city's evolution from Neolithic times through to Roman settlement, the Byzantine era and the early Middle Ages. Highlights include a model of the Roman forum, an impressive collection of glassware and artifacts from the Liburnian period (see p31).

Top 10 Public Statues

1 Grgur Nin, Nin
Ivan Meštrović's larger-than-life bronze monument to 10th-century cleric Bishop Gregory of Nin.

2 Grgur Nin, Split
Another colossal image of Gregory of Nin, who campaigned for Mass to be conducted in Croatian.

3 Marko Marulić, Split
Meštrović's homage to the 15th-century Split-born writer often dubbed "the father of Croatian Literature".

4 Street Art, Split
Look out for the giant teacup on Marmontova and the new silver bridge on the Riva.

5 Orlando's Column, Dubrovnik
Standard-bearer for the Divine Republic, Orlando flies the Libertas flag of the Dubrovnik Festival in summer (see p11).

6 Ivan Gundulić, Dubrovnik
Characteristically oversized Meštrović statue, honouring the life and work of this local 17th-century poet.

7 Juraj Dalmatinac, Pag Town
A lifelike statue of the man who designed Pag Town.

8 Franjo Tuđman, Pridriga
A giant statue of the former Croatian president takes centre stage in this small town, which was decimated during the war of the early 1990s (see p35).

9 Juraj Dalmatinac, Šibenik
The architect keeps a watchful eye on the cathedral he didn't live to see completed.

10 Father Andrija Kačić Miošić, Makarska
Impressive tribute to this 18th-century priest and poet.

In Croatian addresses, "bb" is short for bez broj, meaning "without number".

41

Left **Prižna Bay, Lumbarda** Right **Zlatni Rat, Brač**

🔟 Beaches

1 Zlatni Rat, Brač
The "Golden Cape" – a popular sweep of fine shingle that curls out, lapped by the currents of the Adriatic, from the pine-fringed southern flank of the island of Brač – is much eulogized, and photos of this distinctive landmark near the resort of Bol are, deservedly, omnipresent in holiday brochures ◈ *Map E5*

2 Orebić
You couldn't wish for a more spectacular location to unfurl your towel than the beach of this small resort, with its collage of fine shingle and sand. Across the water, on the very tip of the Pelješac Peninsula, you can see the terracotta roof tiles of Korčula Town, as starched mountainscapes embrace all around *(see p91)*. ◈ *Map H1*

3 City Beach, Dubrovnik
The sand may be imported, and there's an entry charge to the section with sun loungers,

but the sweeping views of old Dubrovnik are hard to beat, the waters are clean, and the island of Lokrum tempts offshore. ◈ *Map K5*

4 Pakleni Islands, Hvar
The "Islands of Hell" may not sound too inviting, but this necklace of tiny islands just off Hvar provides plenty of great places to laze by the sea. A short boat trip from Hvar Town and you find yourself sitting by the Adriatic with very little in the way of tourist development to spoil the surroundings. Clothes are very much optional on Jerolim. ◈ *Map D6*

5 Nin
The Northern Dalmatian town of Nin is renowned as a site of religious and historical importance, but it's also surrounded by real sand beaches, something of a rarity in the region. Development remains low-key, and when the wind blows in strongly from the Velebit mountains the waters are best left to windsurfers, but on a hot summer's day there are few better places to be *(see p74)*. ◈ *Map B3*

6 Telašćica Nature Park
Framed around the epic sweep of Telašćica Bay, this nature park on Dugi Otok is currently being reforested after a serious

City Beach, Dubrovnik

fire in 1995. There are plenty of little nooks and crannies where you can search for your own bit of paradise, but beware visiting yachts that tend to venture into isolated coves when you least expect it. Note that facilities are rather limited. Map B4

Gradac

The small town of Gradac boasts the longest beach in Croatia, and the best on the Makarska Riviera. Shingle and pebbles abound along the tree-fringed shoreline. Out to sea, the island of Hvar looms on the horizon. Some sections of the beach offer tourist facilities; others are far more rustic. In summer it can be tricky to find a secluded spot (see p82). Map J1

Zrće, Novalja, Pag

Not quite yet the "Croatian Ibiza" it aims to become, this sweep of sand and shingle set apart from the resort of Novalja is nonetheless spectacular, with the starched scenery of Pag all around and the Velebit mountains rising in the background. Three large nightclubs, beach bars, and fast-food outlets fail to spoil the scenery of a beach that feels pretty remote from just about everywhere. Map A2

Prižna Bay, Lumbarda

While chocolate-box beauty Korčula Town gets all the plaudits, the nearby town of Lumbarda has much better beaches. Prižna Bay has a decent sandy beach with a sprinkling of cafés in a very low-key scene. Buses run daily from Korčula Town, while in

Gradac, Makarska Riviera

summer there are boats as well. If Prižna Bay gets a little too crowded for your liking, nearby Bilin Žal tends to be a bit quieter. Map H2

Koločep

Just a short ferry-ride from Dubrovnik, the island of Koločep has a good sandy beach, which is usually a lot quieter than the ones in and around the city. This is not a glitzy resort or family-friendly oasis – just a quiet and unassuming spot for those looking to venture off the beaten track (see p95). Map K2

Left **Hiking** Right **Scuba diving**

Outdoor Activities

Windsurfing
Windswept coastlines near Nin, on Brač, and along the Pelješki Channel (Korčula and Pelješac) are all popular haunts for windsurfers ◈ *Orca Sport: www.orca-sport.com • Perna: www.perna-surf.com*

Windsurfing

Rafting
Adrenaline-fuelled white-water rafting trips are becoming increasingly popular, with a number of operators organizing trips on the Cetina River. Trips generally last from three to four hours, and take place on the lower stretch of this 105-km-(65-mile-) long waterway, around 20 minutes from the coastal town of Omiš *(see p83)*. ◈ *Huck Finn: www.huck-finn.hr*

Rafting

Scuba Diving
Dive schools along the Dalmatian coast offer trial dives, diving courses, equipment hire, night dives and wreck dives. Some of the best diving can be done with Biševo's Blue Grotto *(see p84)* from the island of Vis, where there are myriad offshore wrecks. Contact the Croatian

Diving Federation for more information. ◈ *Croatian Diving Federation: www.diving-hrs.hr*

Sea Kayaking
This is a sport that experts expect to take off in a big way over the coming years, with the majority of trips centred around Dubrovnik and the Elafiti Islands. You can take anything from a short excursion to a week-long break. Local travel agencies in Dubrovnik can organize sea-kayaking tours.

Climbing
The vaulting peaks of the Biokovo, Dinaric and Velebit mountain ranges have an irresistible allure to mountaineers, who flock here from all over Europe. Paklenica National Park is well set up for climbers; bolted routes offer a wide variety of challenges on the lower slopes, while free climbing is also possible.

Walking and Hiking
Dalmatia has an almost infinite number of walking and hiking opportunities, from easy, low-level walks to steep ascents requiring a higher level of fitness. Seek local advice, and ensure that you have the right equipment. UK-based Headwater organize walking holidays around the Dalmatian coast. ◈ *Headwater: www.headwater.com*

Tennis
7 National heroes Goran Ivanišević, Mario Ančić and Karolina Šprem have all fuelled Croatia's love of tennis. Public courts can be found near resort hotels and towns throughout Dalmatia. One of the region's most famous courts is in the Bačvice area of Split, where Ivanišević trained as a youngster.

Swimming
8 Given Croatia's lengthy coastline, it's hardly surprising that swimming is a popular outdoor sport. Those not keen to swim in the sea will find enclosed pools near the waterfronts in Korčula, Split and Šibenik, amongst others.

Snorkelling
9 Cheap and easy, with a bountiful coastline to choose from; just don a mask and flippers, and you're away.

Picigin, Split
10 A summer sport peculiar to Split, picigin is more about posing than point-scoring. Head to Bačvice *(see p25)*, stand in the sea with a small black rubber ball, wearing your best swimwear and designer sunglasses, throw the ball nonchalantly then catch it with one hand, and you will blend in with the Spličani.

Picigin

Top 10 Spectator Sports

1 Football
Dalmatians are passionate about football. Football shirts and the graffiti of their fans (known as the Torcida) attest to the fact that most support premier-division Hajduk Split.

2 Basketball
Dalmatia's most famous stars, Dražen Petrović and Krešimir Ćosić (now both sadly deceased), fuelled the nation's dedication to the sport.

3 Tennis
Because Croatia has its own home-grown tennis celebrities, Croatians like to watch the game as much as they like to play it.

4 Sailing
Regular regattas and boat shows have made sailing more than just a participant sport.

5 Beach Volleyball
During peak season, beach volleyball matches spring up along the Makarska Riviera.

6 Water Polo
A strong national team has secured water polo a sizable following.

7 Bočanje
A popular sport similar to the French game *pétanque*.

8 Extreme Sports
Brač's annual extreme sports festival is held in July each year. Enjoy free climbing, windsurfing, skating, biking, paragliding, and more.

9 Handball
Handball has surged in popularity since Croatia won gold at the 2004 Olympics.

10 Rowing
The Skelin brothers from Split took silver at the 2004 Olympics. Most Dalmatian towns have a rowing club.

Left **Hvar Town** Right **Sailing in the Kornati Islands**

Sailing Routes

Dubrovnik–Korčula
This southern-Adriatic route eases its way from Dubrovnik *(see pp8–15, 58–66)* to Koločep, Lopud, Šipan *(see p95)* and Mljet *(see p92)*. From the Mljet National Park, head up the Pelješki Channel en route to Korčula Town *(see pp16–17)*. A detour from Šipan to Ston, from where you can walk to Mali Ston *(see p92)* and savour first-rate Adriatic fish, is well worth it.

Split–Vis
Many yachts make a beeline for Brač and Hvar, and miss out on the beauty of Šolta (much favoured by the Spličani) and Vis. Hvar certainly has its attractions, though – not least, plenty of secluded coves flanked by impressive mountains *(For Brač, Hvar, Šolta and Vis, see p84)*.

Sailing from Split to Vis

Split–Dugi Otok
This stunning though less well-trodden route takes sailors from Split *(see pp24–5)* to Šolta, Rogoznica *(see p76)* and Žirje, then into the Kornati Islands archipelago *(see pp26–7)*, where Piškera has a good marina. From here, make the journey to Dugi Otok before returning by way of Primošten *(see p74)*, which has become quite a hub for sailors in recent years.

Murter–Kornati Islands
The sheltered nature of the Kornati archipelago is a virtual guarantee of calm weather, making the Kornatis a favourite haunt of novice or inexperienced sailors, as well as learn-to-sail course operators.

Zadar Archipelago
At the height of summer, when the Kornatis are crowded, the Zadar Archipelago, with over 200 islands, offers sailors a more tranquil alternative. *(For Dugi Otok, Silba, Pašman, Ugljan and Iž, see p77.)*

Šibenik Archipelago
If you want to be able to find secluded bays at any time of year, try the islands near Šibenik. Highlights include Žirje, Privić *(see p77)*, Kaprije, Tijat, Obonjan and Zlarin. Zlarin (the closest to Šibenik) is particularly appealing; cars are banned, and residents still rely on the land and sea for a living (agriculture, fishing, sponge-diving and wine-making are its key industries).

Trogir–Lastovo
Watch enviously from Trogir marina *(see pp18–19)* as the millionaires moor up on the Riva before heading due south to Brač, Hvar *(see p84)*, Korčula

The usually calm Croatian waters are perfect for beginners. Neilson (www.neilson.co.uk) arrange "learn to sail" flotilla holidays.

(see pp16–17, 95) and Lastovo (see p95). For a real Robinson Crusoe experience, be sure to explore the islets to the northeast – Česvinica, Kručica, Stomoria and Saplon. Saplon has the added bonus of sand beaches.

Trogir–Dubrovnik

Be warned: this is a trip for serious sailing enthusiasts, with big distances between stops. Starting from Trogir, the route takes in Hvar, Vis, Vela Luka (Korčula), Mljet and Dubrovnik.

The island of Pag

Zadar–Rab

Leave the Zadar archipelago behind and search out the island of Pag (see pp37, 77), with its ghostly beauty and empty bays. From Pag, break away from Dalmatia altogether and explore the neighbouring island of Rab in the Kvarner Gulf, where the picture-perfect Rab Town is a highlight not to be missed.

Split–Dubrovnik

An extended one-way charter allows a thorough exploration of central and southern Dalmatia taking in Split, Trogir, Šolta, Brač, Hvar, Vis, Korčula, Mljet and Dubrovnik. Take the time to explore islands and islets, like Pakleni Otok (see pp42, 84) and the islands around Mljet's Polače Bay. This route also allows an exploration of more than one settlement on each island.

Top 10 Sailing Tips

1 Know the Rules
Before you sail, check the local rules of navigation with the Association of Nautical Tourism. ◈ Bulevar Oslobođenja 23, 51000 Rijeka • 051 209 147

2 Join a Flotilla
Consider joining a flotilla; shorter distances and tuition make them ideal for beginners.

3 Reputable Operators
Adriatic Holidays, Sunsail and Cosmos Yachting are all well-established businesses. ◈ www.adriaticholidaysonline.com • www.sunsail.com • www.cosmosyachting.com

4 Charter a Skipper
He or she will know the waters, and may even cook.

5 Vital Documentation
Make sure that you have certified crew and passenger lists, as well as proof that the boat is seaworthy, has third-party insurance, and that you are authorized to sail it.

6 Pre-book Marinas
From June to September, mooring space is at a premium.

7 Sail During the "Shoulder" Season
For good weather without the summer crowds, May and September are best.

8 Weather Forecasts
Check the weather on your VHF radio. For Dubrovnik the frequency is 73; for Split, 67.

9 Pack Sparingly
It's surprising how many beginners try to fit six huge suitcases on board; remember that space is at a premium.

10 Annual Berths
If you are planning to berth your boat in Croatia long-term, consider joining the ACI (Adriatic Croatia International Club). ◈ www.aci-club.hr

Skippered boats can be hired from companies such as Sunsail (see above) and Hidden Croatia (www.hiddencroatia.com).

Left **Adio Mare, Korčula** Right **Stellon, Split**

🔟 Restaurants

1 Vila Kaliopa, Vis Town
This enchanting restaurant is set in the midst of an elegant sculpture garden. The fish could not be fresher, and the service is every bit as stylish as the surrounds *(see p87)*.

Vila Kaliopa, Vis Town

2 Vila Koruna, Mali Ston
Dine on oysters and mussels plucked straight from the waters in front of the restaurant. With fish and shellfish this fresh, you may prefer them to be served simply, but the restaurant is equally adept at conjuring up dishes with that extra touch of flair *(see p97)*.

3 Adio Mare, Korčula Town
This bustling seafood restaurant is located in the old quarter of Korčula Town, close to the reputed birthplace of Marco Polo. Fragrant smoke billows from the fish grill, beckoning in the crowds – but despite the volume of diners, the restaurant manages to maintain the quality, and few leave unsatisfied *(see p97)*.

4 Zlatna Ribica, Brodarica
Business types flock here to impress their clients, and it is easy to see why. Fresh fish is the speciality of this upscale restaurant, with a feast of *langoustines*, grilled platters and *brodet* (fish stew served with polenta) complemented by fine wines and a stunning view over the island of Krapanj *(see p79)*.

5 Foša, Zadar
The interior is nothing special, but the location – by the sea, looking up towards Zadar's old town walls – is fabulous. The terrace is a divine place to relax and enjoy plump grilled squid on a warm day *(see p79)*.

6 Stellon, Split
Fine restaurants are thin on the ground in Split, but this popular bolthole in the Bačvice complex manages to please many tastes. For those not keen on seafood, there's steak with blue cheese and truffle sauce, or for lunch, pizza baked in a wood-fired oven *(see p87)*.

7 Nostromo, Split
Nostromo is the best place to eat in the centre of town. It's just by the fish market, so the seafood is about as fresh as it gets. The decor is light and airy – a refreshing change from nautical theming *(see p87)*.

Fish platter, Nostromo, Split

8 Taverna Rustica, Dubrovnik

Part of the Excelsior Hotel but breaking the traditional hotel-restaurant mould, this cosy retreat beyond the Ploče Gate has a snug "couples" area, where diners just call when they need a waiter. Cuisine-wise, the emphasis is on stylishly prepared (and none too rustic) Dalmatian fish and meat specialities. If the conversation falters, the stunning views of the old town should be a good talking point (see p69).

9 Atlas Club Nautika, Dubrovnik

Long the most famous restaurant in the city, Atlas Club Nautika has many would-be detractors, but it usually hits the spot for most diners. The menu nods towards the Adriatic, but there are also meat and vegetarian dishes. Vying for centre stage, though, are the wonderful views, with the old town to one side and Lovrijenac Fortress to the other (see p69).

Restaurant Fontana, Trogir

10 Restaurant Fontana, Trogir

Unlike many restaurants on the Dalmatian coast, the Fontana – the best restaurant in Trogir – stays open year round. In winter it retreats to a cosy interior; in the warmer months it explodes out onto the waterfront Riva. The speciality, unsurprisingly, is seafood (see p87).

Top 10 Culinary Highlights

1 Adriatic Platter
A generic term for a feast of Adriatic fish and shellfish, usually grilled *(na žaru)*, and served with garlic, lemon, potatoes and mangold *(blitva)*.

2 Ston Oysters *(Oštrige)*
Head to Mali Ston for divine oysters straight from the beds just offshore.

3 Pag Cheese *(Paški Sir)*
Pag produces a distinctive salted sheep's cheese – the finest cheese in the country.

4 Seafood Risotto *(Rižot)*
You will find this dish featured on menus up and down the coast – a good-value meal.

5 Dalmatian Ham *(Pršut)*
This air-dried smoked ham, often served as a starter with Pag cheese, is arguably better than the Italian equivalent.

6 Pag Lamb *(Janjetina)*
Flavoursome lamb from the parched isle where the lambs feed on fresh herbs.

7 Lobster *(Jastog)*
Diners can often select their own lobster from the tank, usually served simply.

8 Grilled Squid *(Lignje na Žaru)*
Fresh squid grilled with garlic and garnished with squeezed lemon makes a delicious starter or main course.

9 Istrian Truffles *(Tartufi)*
From Croatian Istria, both white and black varieties are often a match for French and Italian truffles.

10 Scampi *(Buzara)*
This rich and flavoursome seafood dish is a Dalmatian speciality. Scampi are gently simmered in a sauce of tomato, onion and herbs.

For more restaurant listings **See pp68, 69, 79, 87, 97**

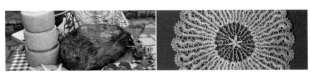

Left *Paški sir* (Pag cheese) and *Pršut* (smoked ham) Right **Lace**

🔟 Things to Buy

1 Ties

Its original name – "cravat" – may be French, but the tie comes from Croatia. During the Thirty Years' War, the French cavalry noticed that Croatians wore their scarves in a distinctive manner – which they termed *à la cravate* ("Croatian-style"). Quality ties can be bought in Croata shops in Dubrovnik, Split and Cavtat.

2 Wine

Quality Dalmatian wines include the reds Plavac, Dingač and Postup from the Pelješac Peninsula. Grk and Pošip (white) are grown in Korčula. Vineyards in the Konavle region produce delectable Dubrovačka Malvazija (also white). Outside of Dalmatia, Žlahtina from the island of Krk, Graševina from Slavonia, and Istrian Malvazija – again all white – are also excellent. It's best to buy direct from the vineyard – otherwise, from a *Vinoteka* (wine shop).

Dingač wine

3 Croatian Spirits

Dalmatians are fond of grape-, herb- and plum-based brandies like *grappa*, *travarica* and *šljivovica*, which are drunk as aperitifs or digestifs. *Grappa* is an Italian spirit made from the leftovers of the winemaking process. Travarica and Šljivovica are both types of *rakija*, powerful spirits made by distillation of fermented fruits. Nicely packaged bottles crammed with herbs make good gifts.

4 Jewellery

Dalmatia is particularly well known for its red Adriatic corals and its jewellery. The quality and price of goods depend on the vendor. Upmarket boutiques in Hvar Town are reliable outlets for contemporary coral pieces. Jewellers in Zadar and Dubrovnik are good for silver and gold.

5 Food

Paški sir (Pag cheese), *pršut* (air-dried smoked ham), olive oil and honey are all first-rate food products. If you can, buy direct from locals (look out for the handmade signs displayed on the roadside), or from fresh-food markets. Failing that, you will also find these items in supermarkets and tourist shops.

6 Dolls in Traditional Costume

Dolls in traditional dress are ubiquitous throughout Dalmatia. There are dozens of varieties, from cheap and cheerful souvenirs to figures wearing handmade clothes. Ceramic dolls offer a more contemporary take on this customary memento.

7 Lace

Lace products come in many guises, including tablecloths, handkerchiefs and clothing, and can be bought in boutiques throughout Dalmatia. If you are looking for something really

For more on Dalmatian wine **See p106**

authentic, buy intricate hand-woven lace made by Pag islanders, or pick up a piece crafted by nuns in Hvar Town using the leaves of agave plants, which grow on the island.

Lavender
This fragrant plant has been cultivated on Hvar for the past 75 years, and the myriad oils and balms that are produced provide an important source of revenue for the islanders. In late spring and early summer, the scent of lavender pervades the island, and a host of products are sold at stalls around Hvar Town.

Lavender stall, Hvar

Clothing and Accessories
Dalmatians take great pride in their appearance, and boutique shops in the historic cores of Dubrovnik, Split and Zadar, are great places to purchase stylish clothes and leather goods – especially shoes and handbags.

Handicrafts
Croatia has a long tradition of ceramics and wooden handi-crafts. Nautically-themed goods are common in Split, as well as replicas of Meštrović sculptures. In Dubrovnik, you can pick up dolls, wooden toys and ceramic hearts – the latter harking back to the times when the families of seafaring men would donate gold or silver hearts to churches, as votive offerings to ensure the safe return of their loved ones.

Top 10 Tips for Buying Art and Crafts

1 Artur Galerija, Dubrovnik
Come here for images of the Old City. ✪ Lučarica 1 • Map J5

2 Dubrovačka Kuća, Dubrovnik
A quality gift shop and art gallery (see p63).

3 Gallery Stradun, Dubrovnik
If you're looking for depictions of Dubrovnik and Dalmatia, this is the place. Discounts for cash. ✪ Placa bb • Map H5

4 Sebastian, Dubrovnik
This newly refurbished gallery with a history dating back over 30 years sells quality work by famous artists from former Yugoslavia. ✪ Svetog Dominika 5 • Map K5

5 Arsia, Split
Arsia sells decent Meštrović replicas, and paintings of Split. ✪ Dioklecijanova 3 • Map Q2

6 Dioklecijanova, Split
This street leading south from the Golden Gate is home to a handful of good craft studios. ✪ Map Q2

7 Diocletian's Palace, Split
The souvenir stalls in the Main Hall stock a wide selection of art (see p22).

8 Gallery Anima, Zadar
Paintings of Dalmatia by local artist Zoran Debelić. ✪ Plemića Borelli 16 • Map B3

9 Gallery More, Zadar
Located on the old town's main street, with a good range of typical Croatian gifts. ✪ Široka bb • Map B3

10 Gallery Pia, Zadar
Ceramics, textiles and paintings by locally and nationally known artists. ✪ Jadro 9 • Map B3

In Croatian addresses, "bb" is short for bez broj, meaning "without number".

51

Left **Stradun, Onoforio's fountain** Right **Sea kayaking**

Children's Dalmatia

Beaches
Sandy beaches may be few and far between, but Dalmatia boasts long stretches of clean, sun-kissed pebble and shingle beach. Even at the height of summer, you will find whole swathes of shoreline deserted. On busy public beaches, snack bars, sun loungers and parasols are common – some even have changing rooms and showers.

Wooden walkways, Krka National Park

Public Swimming Pools
They may not be plush, but Dalmatia has some of the best-located public swimming pools in Europe, allowing parents to enjoy views of places such as Korčula Old Town, the island of Šolta (from Split) and the bay at Šibenik while the kids take a dip.

Fortifications and Towers
Dalmatia overflows with towers and fortifications offering stunning views. Lather on the

Ferry, Split to Vis

sunscreen and carry plenty of water. Cafés located along the way to high vantage points, at the top of towers, and in the fortifications themselves, help ease the strain for shorter legs.

Krka National Park
This fun-filled natural wonderland should keep everyone happy, with lush vegetation, thundering waterfalls, imposing monuments and a maze of wooden walkways – not to mention boat rides and the chance to take a dip in the water *(see pp21–2)*.

Paklenica National Park
Deliberately manicured for tourists, the lower levels of Velika Paklenica have ascents with solid paths that are quite manageable for older children. Information boards document the park's wildlife and fauna. The calm waters that hug the beaches of the nearby resort at Starigrad are also perfect for kids *(see p73)*.

Ferries
The whole length of the Dalmatian coast is awash with catamarans and ferries of all shapes and sizes, transforming a sightseeing visit to an island into a sea-borne adventure. It's best to leave the car behind at the height of the summer.

For more on Dalmatia's beaches **See pp42–3**

Resort Hotels

The swimming pools, tennis courts and other leisure facilities at resort-style hotels will keep kids happily occupied for hours. Full- and half-board options are worth considering, particularly with younger children.

Swimming pool, Dubrovnik Palace Hotel

Cycling

Once you get away from the busy highways and tourist resorts, Dalmatia is replete with cycling opportunities. Many hotels and campsites rent bikes to guests; some provide them free of charge.

Adventure Sports

If your older children crave a little excitement, adrenaline-pumping white-water rafting, sea kayaking, river canoeing, sailing, mountain biking and organized hiking trips can be arranged at local travel agencies.

International Children's Festival

For a fortnight every year (June to July), stages and public squares in the historic city of Šibenik (see p73) host lively children's theatre, music and puppet shows. A tradition that spans almost half a century, the International Children's Festival appeals to younger children, Croatian and non-Croatian alike. There's also an art programme, including children's workshops.

Top 10 Children's Attractions

1 City Beach, Dubrovnik
The banana boat rides are always a popular distraction in summer (see p42).

2 Croatia's "Dead Sea"
Children are delighted to find they can float with ease in the salt waters of the Mrtvo More, a sea-fed lake on the island of Lokrum (see p94).

3 Biševo Grotto
On a sunny day, nothing is more spectacular (see p84).

4 Beach Activities, Hvar
The beach just outside the Amphora Hotel is a good place to hire snorkelling equipment and mountain bikes (see p84).

5 Spanish Fort, Hvar Town
This 16th-century fort is a firm favourite with all ages, and the young ones can burn off some energy on the steep ascent.

6 Split Football Stadium
Treat them to some thrilling soccer action at the home of premier-division Hajduk Split.
● www.hnkhajduk.hr

7 Roman Ruins, Salona
Stimulate their imaginations with a visit to this fascinating archeological site (see p81).

8 St Ana Fort, Šibenik
The kids can maraud around this ancient fortification while you take in the stunning views (see p73).

9 Zvonimira, Zadar
The coastline stretching south-east from the old town has pleasant wooded parks, and beaches with bathing areas and diving boards.

10 Puppet Theatre, Zadar
If wet weather spoils your plans, check out this fun venue.
● Obala Kralja Tomislava bb
● 023 319 181

For more on outdoor activities See pp44–5

Left **Split Summer Festival** Right **Dubrovnik Festival**

🔟 Festivals & Events

1 Feast of St Blaise, Dubrovnik

On 3 February, the citizens of Dubrovnik commemorate the life and work of their patron saint and protector *(see p38)*. The celebrations begin at 10am, with a mass held outside the cathedral. At 11:30am, reliquaries of St Blaise are carried in a procession around the city.

Feast of Saint Blaise celebrations

2 Carnival

Spectacular Shrove Tuesday carnival processions take place in Split, where masked locals burn an effigy of Krnjo, a mythical figure representing everything bad that has happened to the city over the previous year. On the same day, in a celebration known as Poklad, the inhabitants of Lastovo commemorate a 15th-century victory of the islanders over pirates; a puppet is chased, captured and burned at the stake.

3 Dubrovnik International Film Festival

This relatively new five-day event has screenings of a wide range of Croatian and international films. ◈ www.dubrovnikiff.org • May

4 Zadar Summer Theatre

This lively festival of theatre, music and dance was founded in 1995. Most of the productions take place in a variety of outdoor locations around the old city. ◈ Jul–Aug

5 Musical Evenings in St Donat's Church, Zadar

Every summer, St Donat's Church *(see p31)* and other ecclesiastical venues in Zadar come alive with a host of Baroque, Renaissance, medieval and chamber concerts. ◈ www.kuz.hr • mid-July–mid-Aug

6 Dubrovnik Festival

For over 50 years, stages in historic venues, churches and the open air have filled the old city with theatre, dance and music from around the globe. Performances of Shakespeare in the Lovrijenac Fortress sell out quickly. ◈ www.dubrovnik-festival.hr • mid-Jul–late Aug

Musical evenings in St Donat's Church

Split Summer Festival

Opera, ballet, classical music, pop, and a diverse array of theatrical performances heighten the energy in Dalmatia's largest city. Open-air productions held in Diocletian's Palace (see pp22–3) are the highlight, with the staging of Verdi's *Aida* in the Peristyle an enduring favourite. ◈ www.splitsko-ljeto.hr • mid-Jul–late Aug

Traditional swords and shield of the Moreška

Moreška, Korčula Town

This traditional 15th-century sword-dance, staged in Korčula Town on the Feast of St Theodore (29 July), portrays good and evil kings fighting for the affections of a beautiful maiden. Though the swords are wooden, the battles are spectacularly choreographed.

Summer Festivals

In July and August, summer festivals lasting anything from two weeks to two months fill the cultural calendars of many towns throughout Dalmatia, with dance, theatre and music gracing outdoor and indoor stages. Some of the liveliest festivals are held in Cavtat, Hvar Town, Makarska, Ston, Trogir and Pag.

Split Jazz Festival

This week-long festival runs during the city's Summer Festival, bringing international jazz performers of the calibre of Diana Krall, Charlie Haden and Michael Brecker to the Dalmatian capital. ◈ Aug

Top 10 Venues

1 Martin Držić Theatre, Dubrovnik
Ornate venue staging a wide-ranging theatrical programme. ◈ Pred Dvorom 3 • 020 321 088

2 Rector's Palace, Dubrovnik
Classical concerts are staged in the open-air atrium from April to October (see pp14–15).

3 Sponza Palace, Dubrovnik
Atmospheric venue in the inner courtyard of this 16th-century palace (see p11).

4 Church of St Saviour, Dubrovnik
This old-town church hosts classical concerts every Monday at 9pm (see p11).

5 Town Theatre, Hvar
One of Europe's earliest theatres. ◈ Trg Svetog Stjepana • 021 741 009

6 Open Air Theatre, Korčula Town
This compact circular arena overlooks the harbour and the Pelješac Peninsula.

7 Fort of St Nicholas, Šibenik
In season, a flotilla of boats ferries concertgoers to the fort from Šibenik (see p76).

8 Šibenik Theatre
This grand venue was modelled on Venice's Teatro Fenice. ◈ Kralja Zvonimira 1 • 022 213 145

9 Croatian National Theatre, Split
Impressive theatre hosting opera, ballet and classical music performances. ◈ Trg Gaje Bulata • 021 515 999

10 Croatian National Theatre, Zadar
This opulent venue hosts theatre, opera and ballet. ◈ Široka 8 • 022 314 552

You can see Moreška dancing throughout the main summer season in Korčula Town.

55

AROUND DUBROVNIK & THE DALMATIAN COAST

TOP 10 OF DUBROVNIK & THE DALMATIAN COAST

Left **Old Harbour** Right **Recital at the Rector's Palace**

Dubrovnik

BYRON CALLED IT "THE PEARL OF THE ADRIATIC". *George Bernard Shaw proclaimed that "Those who seek paradise on earth should seek it in Dubrovnik."* Now fully recovered from the bitter Serbian and Montenegrin siege of 1990–91, this remarkable former city-state has in its historic centre perhaps the most attractive and well preserved Baroque core of any European city, its swathe of churches, palaces and old stone houses neatly contained within the sturdy walls that have protected its famed libertas (freedom) for centuries. Much of what you see today is the result of painstaking reconstruction after the earthquake of 1667; now, all new building work is strictly controlled, even down to the shade of green to be used on the shutters of the city's main thoroughfare, the Stradun.

🔟 Sights

1	Stradun and City Walls	**6**	Old Harbour
2	Dominican Monastery	**7**	War Photo Limited
3	Cathedral	**8**	Museum of Modern Art
4	Church of St Blaise	**9**	Sponza Palace
5	Rector's Palace	**10**	Lovrijenac Fortress

City walls

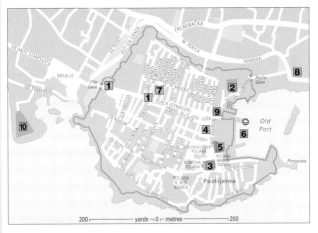

Preceding pages **Hvar Town, island of Hvar**

Stradun and City Walls

There are few better ways to begin your exploration of Dubrovnik than a stroll down the Stradun or a walk around the city walls (see pp8–11).

Dominican Monastery

The Dominicans were allowed into the city in the 14th century, on condition that they helped to protect its southern entrance. The monastery buildings that you see today – the large church, cloisters and museum – were constructed from scratch after the original complex was more or less flattened by the earthquake of 1667. Highlights include the Gothic cloisters, 14th-century Italian painter Paolo Veneziano's *Crucifixion* (in the church), and the museum, which houses an 11th-century Bible and a painting by Titian, *St Blaise, St Mary Magdalene, the Angel Tobias and the Purchaser* – the man on his knees in the latter is a member of the then powerful Pučić family, who funded the work. ✆ *Svetog Dominika 4 • Map K4 • 020 321 423 • 9am–6pm daily • Adm charge*

Crucifixion by Paolo Veneziano

Cathedral

Erected after the 1667 earthquake, today's Baroque cathedral (see p39), crafted by Italian architects, replaced an earlier Romanesque structure. The cathedral houses a treasury with a famous collection of more than 200 reliquaries, including a 12th-century Byzantine case containing the skull of the much venerated St Blaise, and casks containing his hands and one of his legs. It also displays what is claimed to be a fragment of the cross on which Jesus was crucified, and a copy of Raphael's *Virgin of the Chair* reputed to have been made by the grand master himself. ✆ *Poljana Marina Držión • Map J6 • 020 323 459 • 8am–5:30pm, 5–7pm daily • Adm charge*

Skull of St Blaize

Church of St Blaise

The original 14th-century church survived the earthquake largely intact, only to burn down in a fire in 1706. Work started on the present incarnation later the same year, to plans by Italian architect Marino Grapelli, who based the design of the interior on that of a Baroque church in his home town. Punctuating the ornate façade are four pillars watched over by an array of saints. The stained-glass windows are another striking feature – a late-20th-century addition of a kind quite unusual in this part of Europe (see pp11, 38).

Rector's Palace

The position of Rector of Dubrovnik was the ultimate job-share; each incumbent held it for just one month. For that brief period, the Rector's Palace was his home (see pp14–15).

Fall of the Republic

Dubrovnik was always proud of its *libertas*, but on 26 May 1806 it risked it in return for French assistance in lifting a siege by Russian and Montenegrin forces. The French outstayed their welcome, and on 31 January 1808 the Republic of Ragusa was officially dissolved as Dubrovnik became part of Napoleon's "Illyrian Provinces".

Old Harbour

Dubrovnik's first harbour stood to the west side of the city, between the Pile Gate and the Lovrijenac Fortress, but it failed to offer sufficient shelter, and in any case soon became too small as the city grew. The Old Harbour, on the east side of the Old City, is a much grander affair, with the Revelin and St John's forts guarding either flank. Amenities are limited here, but there are one or two places to eat, and take in the busy summer scene; there's always a flurry of small fishing boats and tourist craft enjoying the harbour's protection, and there are good views down the coast towards Cavtat. ◎ *Map K5*

War Photo Limited

Not many tourists make it to this controversial new museum, mistakenly believing that they are going to be presented with a biased depiction of the war in Croatia. In reality, the main

War Photo Limited

exhibit takes an impartial and thought-provoking look at the conflicts that have battered the region since 1991. At the helm is New Zealander Wade Goddard, who has brought together two floors of striking images that don't hold back on shocking detail, but avoid the temptation to label and judge. It is perhaps the ultimate tribute to the gallery that while many Croats feel it is too pro-Serb, many Serbs feel it is too pro-Croat. The gallery itself is a well thought-out space that allows the photographs to speak for themselves. ◎ *Antuninska 6 • Map H4 • 098 367 467 • www.warphoto ltd.com • May–Oct: 9am–9pm daily; Nov–Dec, Mar–Apr: 9am–4pm Mon–Sat (closed Jan, Feb) • Adm charge*

***Olive Trees* by Ignat Job, Museum of Modern Art**

Museum of Modern Art

This avant-garde gallery is housed in an enormous Renaissance-style villa set in a prime spot in affluent Ploče. The light and airy multi-floored venue makes the perfect setting for an eclectic array of permanent and temporary exhibitions. Look out for sculptures by Ivan Meštrović (1883–1962) *(see p40)*, portraits by the Cavtat-born Vlaho Bukovac (1855–1922), and the work of Frano Kršinić (1897–1982), another renowned Croatian sculptor, from Lumbarda in Korčula. ◎ *Frana Supila 23 • Map M5 • 020 426 590 • 9am–9pm daily • Adm charge*

Sponza Palace

Sponza Palace

9 Architect Pasjij Miličević's masterpiece (1506–22) was one of the few buildings to survive the 1667 earthquake. Its exterior presents the onlooker with a striking combination of Gothic and Renaissance architecture. Among the highlights are the flamboyant Gothic windows on the first floor, the Gothic cloisters, and the expert stone carving of brothers Nikola and Josip Andrijić, including a lofty St Blaise who looks down on the Stradun from the second floor *(see p11)*.

Lovrijenac Fortress

10 This sweeping fortress rises steeply out of the Adriatic to the west of the city walls. Historically it served both as a place to store the city's gold and as a military hub and battery where the city could be brought to heel in the event of a rebellion. The city's oft-quoted slogan guards the entrance: "Freedom must not be sold for all the gold in the world". The fortress serves as one of the most atmospheric venues during the Dubrovnik Festival *(see p54)*, with Shakespeare soliloquies echoing across the old ramparts. It's a gruelling climb on a hot day, but well worth the effort. ◎ *Map M5 • 020 324 641 • 9am–6pm daily • Adm charge (no disabled access)*

A Day in Dubrovnik

(Morning)

⏱ If you're an early riser, climb the **city walls** when they open (9am) and you may have them largely to yourself. Make a leisurely circuit taking in their sights *(see pp8–9)* and watching the city as it gradually comes to life below. Stop at **St John's Fort** to visit the **Maritime Museum** *(see p62)* and **Aquarium** *(see p62)*. Descend to the **Stradun**, and if you didn't take breakfast at your hotel, enjoy a coffee and a pastry at the Festival Café *(see p65)* – it's a great vantage-point from which to observe the frenetic street-life of the city's main artery.

Continue strolling gently down the Stradun, just absorbing the atmosphere rather than delving into its various attractions. Enjoy an early seafood lunch at noon in Kamenice *(see p68)* in **Gundulićeva Poljana** *(see p62)*, and absorb the colourful sights and sounds of the market in the same square.

(Afternoon)

After lunch, head across to the **Rector's Palace** *(see pp14–15)* and take a self-guided audio tour. Continue around to the start of the Stradun at **Luža Square**. From here you can choose which of this pedestrianized thoroughfare's attractions to explore *(see pp10–11)* as you travel its length towards the Pile Gate and the welcoming arms of the Kavana Dubravka café *(see p65)*, or perhaps an early dinner at Atlas Club Nautika *(see p69)*, with views over one of Europe's most stunning cities.

Around Dubrovnik

➡ *Take in a concert at the Sponza Palace to see it at its most atmospheric.*

Left **Church of St Ignatius** Right **Gundulić Square**

🔟 Best of the Rest

1 Convent of St Claire
The gleaming orange roof tiles of this former monastery beckon when seen from the Old City walls *(see pp8–9)*. Today it is home to a casual restaurant, Jadran *(see p68)*, set within ornate cloisters. ✪ *Poljana Paksa Miličeva 1 • Map H5*

2 Orthodox Church Museum
Two doors down from the recently refurbished Serbian Orthodox Church is this colourful Icon Museum with works dating from the 15th to 19th centuries ✪ *Od Puča 8 • Map J5 • 020 323 283 • Open 9am–2pm Mon–Sat • Adm charge*

3 Church of St Ignatius
Up a grand sweep of stairs, modelled on Rome's Spanish Steps, is this voluminous 18th-century Jesuit Church. Its dim interior houses fine examples of *trompe l'oeil*. ✪ *Poljana R Boškovića • Map J6 • Open 8am–7pm daily*

4 Pustijerna
Wander the streets of this area to the south of the Stradun in search of traces of the Old City walls. Medieval houses, many in ruins, huddle along impossibly narrow lanes, giving an insight into pre-1667 Dubrovnik. ✪ *Map K6*

5 Synagogue
This little synagogue, up the hill from the Stradun, is said to be Europe's second oldest, after one in Prague. ✪ *Žudioska 5 • Map J5 • Open 10am–3pm Mon–Sat • Adm charge*

6 Gundulićeva Poljana (Gundulić Square)
This beautiful square is home to a statue of Ivan Gundulić, the 17th-century poet whose *Osman* recalls a great Slavic victory over the Turks. There's a lively morning market here. ✪ *Map J5*

7 Aquarium
The Aquarium is a good rainy-day choice, with its poisonous Adriatic moray eels, stingrays, sea horses – and some species also served up in local eateries. ✪ *Damjana Jude 12 • Map K6 • 020 323 978 • Open summer: 9am–9pm daily; winter: 9am–1pm Mon–Sat • Adm charge*

8 Church of St Luke
Renovations spanning nine centuries brought this tiny single-nave church to its present form in 1787. Look out for the saints carved above the main door and the small gallery that is now inside. ✪ *Svetog Dominika bb • Map K4 • 020 321 603 • Opening hours vary*

9 Rupe Ethnographic Museum
This vast space was built to store grain, in holes bored into the rock, in case of siege. The museum looks at daily life over the years. ✪ *Od Rupa 3 • Map H5 • 020 323 013 • Open 9am–6pm daily • Adm charge*

10 Marin Držić House
This museum honours a celebrated 16th-century Dubrovnik playwright. ✪ *Široka 7 • Map H5 • Open 9am–2pm daily • Free*

Left **Croata** Middle **Vinoteka** Right **Dubrovnik House**

🔟 Places to Shop

Art Silver Shop
Stylish bracelets and chunky rings are among the handmade jewellery on sale in this shop. Most are crafted from silver and semi-precious stones.
⬥ *Nalješkovićeva 6 • Map H5*

Dubrovačka Kuća (Dubrovnik House)
This is a charming gallery-cum-gift shop selling quality Croatian wines, Istrian truffles, traditional souvenirs and original paintings.
⬥ *Svetog Dominika bb • Map K4*

Vinoteka
This great little wine shop in the heart of the Old City sells Croatian and Slovenian wines, alongside olive oil and truffles. Despite its misleading address, it is entered from the Stradun.
⬥ *Od Sigurate 2 • Map H4*

Croata
Where better to buy a tie than the country in which they were created? All Croata ties are handmade from silk. Look out also for the branches in Cavtat and Split. ⬥ *Pred Dvorom 2 • Map J5*

Algoritam
This centrally located bookstore is a great place in which to browse through a wide range of fiction and non-fiction foreign language titles. It is also a useful place for visitors wanting to pick up maps, phrase books and Croatian dictionaries.
⬥ *Placa 8 • Map J5*

Tilda
A tiny souvenir shop tucked between the Stradun and Prijeko, Tilda stocks a range of traditional clothes and cloth adorned with intricate hand-embroidery.
⬥ *Zlatarska 1 • Map J5*

La Scarpa
For lovers of handbags and shoes, the handmade leather goods in this small boutique are hard to resist. Reasonably priced belts, wallets and key rings are also on sale. ⬥ *Od Puča 8 • Map J5*

Omega 3
Omega 3's bright, modern costume jewellery makes a great gift for teenagers, while its chic, but affordable, Italian accessories complement a more refined wardrobe. ⬥ *Za Rokom bb • Map G5*

Vinoteka
This large wine shop has a great range of good quality wines from all over Croatia and a decent selection of European vintages too. Attractively bottled spirits and oils are also available. Those searching for the hallowed Istrian truffle can pick up both pastes and oils here. The only downside is the high mark-up.
⬥ *Od Puča 9 • Map J5*

Jagerstar
Designer brands such as Camper, Kickers and Diesel are on sale at this spacious shoe shop. Friendly staff will find your size for you. ⬥ *Od Puča 7 • Map J5*

In Croatian addresses, "bb" is short for bez broj, *meaning "without number".*

Left **Troubadur Hard Jazz Café** Right **Labirint**

🔟 Nightlife

Hemingway Bar
Wicker lounge chairs decked with comfortable cushions offer views of the Rector's Palace and cathedral, ensuring Hemingway's popularity. Buzzing at night, it is shaded and quiet by day. 🗖 *Pred Dvorom bb • Map J5*

Troubadur Hard Jazz Café
Tables at this vibrant bolt hole pour out onto the square behind the cathedral. Regular live music performances keep them full. Don't worry if you can't get a seat as the music can be heard from the neighbouring bars too. 🗖 *Bunićeva Poljana • Map J6*

Latino Club Fuego
Live music, DJs playing Latino to R & B, a chill-out room and a late-evening happy hour (from 10pm to 11pm), not to mention a great location just outside the Pile Gate, all make Fuego popular. 🗖 *Brsalje 8 • Map G4*

Exodus
If you're into dance music and you're staying on the Babin Kuk or Lapad peninsulas, then Exodus is for you. 🗖 *Babin Kuk Hotel Complex, Iva Dulčića 39 • Map L4*

Labirint
In high season this entertainment complex overlooking the old harbour has a small, and fairly expensive, late-night disco. It is the location and the outdoor terrace that you are paying for. 🗖 *Svetog Dominika 2 • Map K5*

Esperanza
This popular nightclub near the bus station caters to a crowd that is into disco and techno. Concerts are also staged here from time to time. 🗖 *Put Republike 30 • Map L4*

Carpe Diem
Tucked inside the Old City Walls *(see pp8–9)* east of the old harbour, this lively bar pumps out the latest tunes. On-street seating is popular, while the interior is modern and comfortable. After a hectic night out, why not return for a more sedate breakfast. 🗖 *Kneza Damjana Jude 4 • Map K6*

Revelin Club
Saturday nights bring a bit of everything at this café-bar's weekly disco, with house music, pop, R & B, rock and Latino grooves all part of the DJ's set. 🗖 *Svetog Dominika bb • Map K4*

Lazereti
An old quarantine house and artisans' workshops now form a venue for traditional folk performances. Keep your eyes peeled for posters, or check with the tourist office to find out what's on. 🗖 *Frana Supila 8 • Map M5*

Klub Orlando
This venue, 10 minutes' walk north of the Old City, attracts a young, grungy crowd with its live music, cult cinema and alternative discos. 🗖 *Branitelja Dubrovnika 41 • Map M4*

The majority of nightclubs in Dubrovnik close by 1am; exceptions include Latino Club Fuego, Labirint, Esperanza and Exodus.

Left **Buža** Right **Cervantes**

Cafés and Bars

Festival Café
At the western end of the Stradun, this café has a mellow and sophisticated air. Director's chairs on the pavement are great for sitting back in and watching the world go by. If you've been hankering after single-malt Scotch whisky, look no further. ◈ *Placa 12 • Map H5*

Buža
On a sunny day follow the signs from Gundulićeva Poljana *(see p62)* to this great open-air bar. Located on the rocks outside the southern Old City Walls, it has great views over the sea to Lokrum. It serves cold drinks only. ◈ *off Od Margarite • Map J6*

Gradska Kavana
Revamped in 2005, this city café has a terrace that is a great place for a spot of people watching. ◈ *Pred Dvorom bb • Map J5*

Kavana Dubravka
The views from this low-key café's terrace are spectacular. It is located between the Pile Gate and the Lovrijenac Fortress. ◈ *Brsalje bb • Map G4*

Cervantes
Sandwiched between the Stradun and Prijeko, this cave-like bar serves the more upmarket wines, like Dingač, by the glass, something that is quite unusual in Croatia. Popular with locals and welcoming to visitors, it also offers tapas. ◈ *Dropčeva 5 • Map J5*

Sunset Bar Hotel
Cocktails and stunning sunset vistas over the Elafiti Islands and Mljet are to be had from the Hotel Dubrovnik Palace's public bar. They more than reward the 15-minute bus journey from Brasilje. ◈ *Masarykov Put 20 • Map K4*

Irish Pub
This buzzing bar, with live football and a lengthy happy hour (from 5pm to 8pm), is popular with English-speakers. ◈ *Od Polača 5 • Map J5*

Gaffe
New to Dubrovnik's bar scene, Gaffe is a more refined version of the Irish theme bar across the street, with a green and dark-wood decor. The staff are friendly and the atmosphere relaxed. ◈ *Od Polača 5 • Map J5*

Netcafe
This contemporary café-bar, with modern flat screens and high-speed Internet access, is a pleasant choice for a drink, even if you don't want to go online. The staff are unfailingly welcoming and helpful. ◈ *Prijeko 21 • Map J4*

Ražonda
Sip delectable Croatian and international vi ntages in the Pučić Palace's elegant wine bar. Be sure to bring some friends, and plenty of cash or a credit card, as the wines are only sold by the bottle. ◈ *Od Puča 1 • Map J5*

In Croatian addresses, "bb" is short for *bez broj*, meaning "without number".

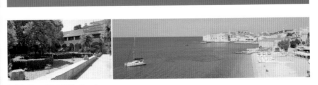

Left **Lokrum** Right **City Beach**

🔟 Beyond the City Walls

1 Gruž Harbour
This increasingly busy harbour, to the north of the Old City, bustles with ferries and cruise ships. It also boasts a cluster of old, Venetian-style palaces. The fresh fruit and vegetable market held every weekday morning is a great place to get a feel for the real Dubrovnik. ⊗ Map L4

2 Mount Srđ
The return of the cable car that used to ascend Mount Srd has been mooted. For now, it is an arduous hike or a drive to the top, to take in the unmatched view of the Old City. ⊗ Map M4

3 Lokrum
Temptingly positioned just offshore is an unspoilt island that is a world away from the city, with quiet coves, an old monastery and a crumbling fort. Boats leave from the old port. ⊗ Map M5

4 City Beach
With great views of the Old City, this beach has recently been revamped, with imported sand and a new bar, restaurant and sun-deck complex. Improvements come at a price, so bring kuna for sun-bed and towel hire. ⊗ Map K5

5 Tuđman Bridge
This graceful bridge provides a suitably grand northern entrance to the city. It also serves as an impressive memorial to the country's first president. ⊗ Map K2

6 Lapad Peninsula
This hotel-laden peninsula retains its beauty through its verdant woodland and has a string of good walking routes. The highest peak, Velika Petka, rises to 192 m (629 ft). ⊗ Map K4

7 Babin Kuk Peninsula
Sharing the same rump of land as Lapad, Babin Kuk is another tree-cloaked peninsula that remains a pleasant area for walking, despite a recent flurry of hotel building. ⊗ Map K4

8 Copacabana Beach
This popular beach offers a range of water sports, from windsurfing and water-skiing to banana-boat rides. You can rent a kayak and explore Babin Kuk from the sea. There are also water-slides for the kids and beach bars for the grown ups. ⊗ Map L4

9 Uvala Bay
The bay that separates Lapad and Babin Kuk boasts its own beach, which was given a make over in the spring of 2005. It is a good spot to while away a sweltering afternoon. ⊗ Map L4

10 Votive Church
The oldest church outside the Old City is dedicated to Dubrovnik's patron saint, St Blaise. A church has stood on the site since at least the 13th century, though today's incarnation dates from the 19th century. ⊗ Gorica Hill, Gruž • Map L4

Atlas Travel Agency (www.atlas-croatia.com) organizes excursions to Montenegro, Mostar and Medugorje.

Tour boat on excursion from Dubrovnik

🔟 Excursions from Dubrovnik

1 Boat Trips
A myriad of tour boats ease their way out into the Adriatic from the old harbour and Gruž, setting course for nearby islands. Short excursions, half-day and day trips are available. ® *Map K5, L4*

2 Scenic Flights
Stunning views unfold on a scenic flight out over the Old City and Lokrum, with options to head north towards Korčula *(see p95)* and the Pelješac Peninsula. ® *Dubrovnik airport • Map L3 • 020 478 674 • www.aer-marina.com*

3 Konavle Safaris
South of Dubrovnik, this unspoilt region offers the chance to get away from it all on an "eco tour". Some operators offer hotel pick up; check with the tourist information office for further details. ® *Map L3*

4 Mlini
This pleasant small fishing village 11 km (7 miles) south of Dubrovnik has a palm-lined water-front and traditional stone houses. Numerous streams, which once fed its mills, and a decent beach add to Mlini's appeal. ® *Map L3*

5 Srebreno
Neighbouring Mlini, Srebreno has a long stretch of beach. It is a low-key resort with two camp-sites and walking and hiking opportunities in the mountains, which protect the village from northerly winds. ® *Map L2*

6 Kotor
Dip south across the border into Montenegro and your reward is the nearest the Adriatic has to a fjord – the stunning Kotor Bay – and the charming historical town of Kotor itself. ® *Map M3*

7 Sveti Stefan
Further on into Montenegro, this hotel is set on its own island and was once a favourite of the international jet set. Today's day-trippers can walk the island and dine in the restaurant. ® *off map*

8 Trebinje
For a taste of a true Bosnian market, nip over the border on a Saturday and enjoy the hectic fun it offers. The centuries peel away in the attractive old town, which boasts mosques and an Orthodox church. ® *Map L2*

9 Mostar
The old bridge that gave the city its name has been expertly restored following its notorious destruction during the 1990s conflict. It is the top sight in this Bosnian city, which lies close to the Croatian border. ® *off map*

10 Međugorje
Even during the war, pilgrims flocked into Bosnia to the spot where the Virgin Mary is said to have appeared to local teenagers in 1981. Facilities catering to hoards of visitors have tainted things a bit, but this is still a remarkable place to visit. ® *Map J1*

Left **Mea Culpa** Middle **Kamenica** Right **Jadran**

Cheap Eats

Mea Culpa
Gargantuan Italian-style pizzas and reasonable prices make Mea Culpa a favourite with locals and visitors alike. Dine in the cosy interior or at a street-side table. ✆ *Za Rokom 3 • Map H5 • 020 323 430 • K*

Sesame
Just east of the Pile Gate, this roof-top terrace is a good place to escape the summer crowds. The food consists of well-prepared Dalmatian dishes. ✆ *Don Frane Bulića 7 • Map M4 • 020 412 910 • KKK*

Kamenice
Gorge on huge plates of fried squid, fresh mussels, seafood risotto and grilled scampi, washed down with a crisp house white. It's great value and the outdoor setting is wonderful. ✆ *Gundulićeva Poljana 8 • Map J5 • 020 323 682 • K*

Jadran
Enjoy fresh Adriatic seafood and simple grilled meats in the attractive courtyard of St Claire's Convent *(see p62)*. Just a stone's throw from the Stradun, the setting is unexpectedly tranquil. ✆ *Poljana Paska Miličevića 1 • Map H5 • 020 429 325 • KKK*

Lokanda Peskarija
Lokanda Peskarija serves a simple menu of mussels, squid, seafood risotto and scampi. Outdoor benches overlook the old harbour, while the rustic interior is atmospheric. ✆ *Na Ponti bb • Map K5 • 020 324 750 • Closed 25 Dec–1 Feb • K*

Poklisar
Decent pizzas and fish main courses are on offer here, but the real reasons for paying a visit to Poklisar are the outdoor tables overlooking the old port and the late opening hours. ✆ *Ribarnica 1 • Map K5 • 020 322 176 • KK*

Arka
One of Dubrovnik's newest restaurants, Arka boasts a varied menu including all the usual Dalmatian fish and meat dishes. Breaking with convention, this informal eatery also has good dedicated vegetarian options. ✆ *Gundulićeva Poljana • Map J5 • KKK*

Fish Sandwich Bar
A tasty selection of fish rolls on home-made bread and portions of fried squid can either be taken away or enjoyed perched on the stools outside. ✆ *Široka bb • Map H5 • K*

Spaghetteria Toni
Located just off the Stradun, this great little trattoria has friendly staff and serves fresh pasta just like *mamma* would make it. ✆ *Nikole Božidarevića 14 • Map H5 • 020 323 134 • K*

Škola
This tiny outlet sells delicious sandwiches created using bread freshly made on the premises and offers unbeatable value. The tasty fillings include cheese, *pršut* and grilled vegetables. ✆ *Antuninska 1 • Map H5 • K*

In Croatian addresses, "bb" is short for bez broj, meaning "without number".

Price Categories

For a three-course meal for one with half a bottle of wine (or equivalent meal), taxes and extra charges.

K	under 100kn
KK	100–150kn
KKK	150–200kn
KKKK	200–250kn
KKKKK	over 250kn

Atlas Club Nautika

🔟 Top-end Restaurants

1 Atlas Club Nautika
Share an Adriatic fish platter or Chateaubriand with a loved one as the Adriatic laps at the rocks below *(see also p49)*. *Brsalje 3 • Map G4 • 020 442 573 • KKKKK*

2 Defne
A roof terrace overlooking the Stradun is home to the summer restaurant of the Pučić Palace. The innovative menu combines Turkish and Croatian cuisine. *Od Puča 1 • Map J5 • 020 326 200 • Closed Oct–May • KKKKK*

3 Victoria Restaurant
The Hotel Argentina's summer restaurant is set on an exclusive terrace below the Villa Orsula. Enjoy a veritable feast as Dubrovnik's old port glitters ahead. *Frana Supila 14 • Map M5 • 020 440 555 • Closed lunch, Oct–May • KKKKK*

4 Taverna Rustica
This romantic retreat nestled in the rocks above the Adriatic has unbeatable views of the Old City. The Dalmatian menu concentrates on seafood; choose your lobster from a tank *(see also p49)*. *Frana Supila 12 • Map M5 • 020 353 353 • Closed lunch, Oct–May • KKKKK*

5 Rozarij
A cosy Old City restaurant in the shadow of the Church of St Nicholas, Rozarij offers tasty grilled meat and fish dishes. *Zlatarska 4 • Map J5 • 020 321 257 • Closed Jan–Mar • KKKK*

6 Proto
Proto shines out above most of the Old City eateries, with a menu that focuses on seafood, but which caters for meat-eaters too. The terrace on the first floor is the place to be in summer. *Široka 1 • Map H5 • 020 323 234 • KKKK*

7 Domino
With a huge hoarding pin-pointing its location, Domino is hard to miss. Dine on succulent steaks on an attractive terrace in atmospheric Pustijerna. *Od Domina 3 • Map H5 • 020 323 103 • KKKKK*

8 Labirint
Savour fish, meat and pasta dishes cooked to perfection, on the most impressive terrace in the Old City, located right up on the ramparts. *Svetog Dominika 2 • Map K4 • 020 322 222 • KKKKK*

9 Hotel Dubrovnik Palace
The refined restaurant at this Lapad hotel is well worth the journey. Excellent regional wines accompany the creative cuisine, and the views over the Elafiti Islands are stunning. *Masarykov Put 20 • Map K4 • 020 430 000 • KKKKK*

10 Villa Dubrovnik
In fine weather, the terrace at Villa Dubrovnik is ideal – right by the sea, with views of the Old City and Lokrum. Chic interior, innovative menu Mediterranean. *Vlahe Bukovac 6 • Map M5 • 020 422 933 • Closed Nov–Apr • KKKKK*

➤ *For more restaurant listings See pp48–9, 79, 87, 97*

Left **Šibenik Old Town** Right **Primošten**

Northern Dalmatia

IN THE KRKA AND KORNATI NATIONAL PARKS, *Northern Dalmatia possesses two of Europe's most stunning natural oases – escapes of breathtaking beauty that enchant everyone from families with children to world-weary travellers. Beyond these two sublime retreats, much of the region is still relatively unexplored, leaving the coastal cities of Zadar and Šibenik relatively free of the tourist crowds. Zadar is a vibrant Adriatic city whose Old Town comes alive in summer with the bustle of pavement cafés and alfresco restaurants, while in the Cathedral of St James, Šibenik boasts one of Europe's most spellbinding cathedrals, as well as a rambling Old Town of its*

own. Elsewhere, surprises such as the trim waterfront towns of Skradin and Novigrad await, and in the extreme north there is Nin, an outpost crucial to early Croatian history, where you will also find some of the best beaches in the land.

Krka National Park

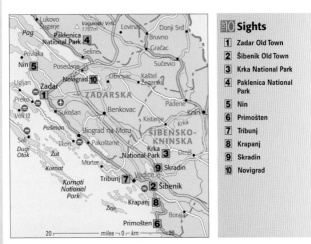

🔟 Sights

1. Zadar Old Town
2. Šibenik Old Town
3. Krka National Park
4. Paklenica National Park
5. Nin
6. Primošten
7. Tribunj
8. Krapanj
9. Skradin
10. Novigrad

Preceding pages **View of Zlatni Rat (Golden Cape), near Bol on the island of Brač**

The Sea Gate, Zadar Old Town

Zadar Old Town
Having hauled itself back from economic meltdown in the 1990s, Zadar is once again a buzzing Adriatic city, complete with an attractive old core which juts out confidently on its own peninsula. This compact and largely pedestrianized area holds the city's main attractions, including a Roman forum and the remarkable Church of St Donat's *(see pp30–31).*

Šibenik Old Town
Given Šibenik's unique position as a city that was founded and developed by the early Croats rather than the Romans or Venetians, it comes as no surprise that its old core is markedly different from the standard Adriatic template. The buildings are smaller, and the streets far narrower and tighter-knit – a real warren, in which it is easy to slip back, in your imagination, through the centuries. In the streets below the castle, forget your map and just wander – but don't miss the Cathedral of St James *(see pp28–9, 37).* ⬡ *Map C4 • Tourist info: Fausta Vrančića 18. 022 212 075*

Krka National Park
This natural playground of pools, waterfalls and emerald lakes makes for a perfect day-trip. On a hot day, bring your swimwear, as the boat that brings you into the park from Skradin drops you off near Skradinski Buk, the best place in the park to cool off in the clear waters of the Krka River. The park is well prepared for tourism, with further boats heading off in search of Visovac Monastery, Krka Monastery and the waterfalls at Roški Slap – not to mention restaurants, cafés, ice cream stalls and souvenir shops *(see pp20–21).*

Paklenica National Park
Designated a national park in 1949, Paklenica has become the destination of choice for savvy Slovene and Italian climbers and walkers. This protected wilderness of vaulting limestone peaks rises from the coast through two sweeping gorges, which just beg to be explored. Velika Paklenica is perfect for day-trippers and walkers, while the more rustic and challenging charms of Mala Paklenica attract serious outdoor types. A network of lodges and mountain huts allows exploration of the higher peaks, though all the usual precautions, as well as local advice, should be taken *(see p52).* ⬡ *Map B2 • Park Office: Franje Tuđmana 14a, Starigrad-Paklenica. 023 369 155. www.paklenica.hr • Adm charge*

Lilies in the Botanical Gardens, Paklenica National Park

For the stunnning Kornati National Park **See pp26–7, 77**

Church of the Holy Cross, Nin

Nin

This small, unassuming town played a major role in Croatia's early history, when it was the political and religious heart of the kingdom. Long ignored by tourists, it is now starting to become more popular – not just for its relaxed ambience, but for its interesting ecclesiastical buildings *(see p38)* and excellent beaches *(see p42)*. The town is easy to explore as a half or full day-trip, and there's a sprinkling of pension-style accommodation. ✪ *Map B3 • Tourist info: Trg Braće Radića 3. 023 265 247. www.nin.hr*

Primošten

Some say that Primošten looks better from a distance than it does close up, but this favourite of the yachting community makes for a very pleasant day-trip, and its hotels invite longer stays. One of the coast's most popular nightclubs, Aurora *(see p78)*, is nearby. ✪ *Map C4 • Tourist info: Rudina Biskupa Josipa Arnerića 2. 022 571 111*

The Road to Independence

Northern Dalmatia was colonized by the Greeks in the 4th century BC. The Romans followed, and it was not until the 10th century that the first Croat state emerged. In 1204, the Venetians took Zadar, and for several centuries they vied with Austria-Hungary for control of the region. The 20th century saw the emergence of Yugoslavia, Mussolini's occupation, and the 35-year dominance of Tito. In 1991 Northern Dalmatia finally became part of an independent Croatia.

Tribunj

On the edge of the Kornati National Park, and connected to the mainland by a bridge, stands the small islet of Tribunj. This is the unlikely base for Dalmatia's largest fishing fleet, and when the catch is landed, it can be an entertaining and colourful place to be. It's a good spot to stop for lunch or an afternoon visit; part of the charm is that you can walk around the whole island in 20 minutes. ✪ *Map C4 • Tourist info: Badnje bb. 022 446 143*

Fisherman mending nets, Tribunj

Krapanj

Just across from the rather unprepossessing mainland village of Brodarica (easily accessed from the Adriatic Highway) lies the picturesque island of Krapanj – the smallest inhabited island in the Adriatic. The trim houses that line the waterfront give way to a small old quarter that is still largely untouched by the incursions of tourism. The only tourist attraction, housed in the Franciscan Monastery, is the Town Museum, which delves into the island's past as a major sponge-diving centre. Boats from Brodarica regularly ply the short route across the channel to the pancake-flat island. ✪ *Map C4*

In Croatian addresses, "bb" is short for bez broj, meaning "without number".

Franciscan Monastery, Krapanj

Skradin

Skradin was on the front line during the wars of the 1990s, and both its Catholic and Orthodox churches took heavy damage during that period. These days the town is prospering, thanks both to its role as a gateway to the Krka National Park *(see pp20–21)*, and to its accessibility as a sailing destination. It's quite a compact little place, and can be walked around in an hour; afterwards, you can reward yourself with lunch or dinner in one of the decent seafood restaurants that are geared towards visiting yachtsmen.
◈ *Map C4 • Tourist info: Trg Male Gospe 3. 022 771 329. www.skradin.hr*

Novigrad

Apart from a well-equipped campsite, tourism has yet really to make its mark on Novigrad. The name means "New Town", so it comes as a pleasant surprise to discover its delightful old core, which meanders off up the hillside. Here, rather than funky pavement-cafés and ice-cream stalls, expect to see card-playing men, and old women hanging out their washing. The best view of the town is from the ruined medieval fortress that looms over it from high on the hillside above. In season, boat trips depart from Novigrad for the nearby Zrmanja Gorge *(see p76)*.
◈ *Map B3 • Tourist info: Obala Elizabete Kotromanić 4. 023 375 051*

A Day in Northern Dalmatia

Morning

Make an early start and head north out of Šibenik to the small town of **Skradin**, where you can have a light breakfast in one of the town's waterfront cafés. From here, you could just take a boat to the **Krka National Park** *(see pp20–21)* and spend the day there. Alternatively, follow the old road which winds its way alongside the new motorway towards Zadar; here, vineyards and new houses are gradually restoring normality to a terrain that not so long ago was ravaged by war.

From the road, you could either drop down to **Lake Vrana** *(see p76)* or just carry straight on for lunch in **Zadar** *(see pp30–31)*. Just outside the old town, Foša *(see pp48, 79)* has a pretty terrace by the water with parking nearby.

Afternoon

After lunch, continue north on the motorway from Zadar. Turn off before the Maslenica Bridge and follow the Novigradsko More east to the compact little town of **Novigrad**, where you can climb the hill to the fortress and enjoy sweeping views out over Northern Dalmatia, before drifting back down to one of the waterfront café-bars, where you can take a break as the local fishing fleet goes about its business. If you're short of time, head straight back to Šibenik; otherwise, make a detour to **Otavice** *(see p76)*, where you can take in the unforgettable family mausoleum of sculptor Ivan Meštrović.

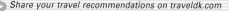

Left **Otavice** Right **Fortress of St Saviour, Knin**

🔟 Best of the Rest

1 Otavice

Ivan Meštrović's stunning family mausoleum overlooks his parents' village. A cubed exterior gives way to an octagonal space graced with delicate religious sculptures. ◈ Map D4 • Open 8–11am, 5–8pm Tue–Sun (summer); 10am–2pm Tue–Sun (winter) • Adm charge

2 Fortress of St Saviour, Knin

The imposing remains of this 10th-century fortress, a crucial defence against the Ottoman Empire, sit high above the bleak town of Knin. ◈ Map D3 • 022 664 822 • Open 8am–4pm daily • Adm charge

3 Rogoznica

This old fishing village, just off the Adriatic Highway between Šibenik and Trogir, has become popular with visiting sailors and holidaymakers. ◈ Map C5 • Tourist office: Kneza Domagoja bb. 022 559 263. www.rogoznica.com

4 Starigrad Paklenica

The gateway to Paklenica National Park (see p73), this town is set dramatically between the Adriatic and the Velebit mountains. ◈ Map B2 • Tourist office: Trg Tome Marasovića 1. 023 369 255

5 Zrmanja Gorge

The spectacular Zrmanja Gorge has been opened up by regular cruises in season from Novigrad. Local operator Flash Touring also runs "canoe safaris" up the gorge. ◈ Map C3 • Flash Touring: 023 375 201

6 Fort of St Nicholas, Šibenik

Guarding the entrance to the channel that leads from the Adriatic into Šibenik, this charming fortress dates back to the 16th century. In summer, concerts are staged here. ◈ Map C4

7 St John's Fortress, Šibenik

This star-shaped fortification, once a bulwark against the Ottomans (it survived a three-week siege in 1647), rises 155 m (508 ft) above sea level. ◈ Map C4

8 Krupa Monastery

Founded in the 17th century by Bosnian monks fleeing the Ottomans, this is the largest Serbian Orthodox monastery in Croatia. ◈ Map C3

9 Biograd Na Moru

An early Croat settlement, Biograd Na Moru is today a low-key resort with an attractive waterfront and a spacious marina. In summer water sports and trips to the Kornati Islands are on offer from here. ◈ Map B3 • Tourist office: Trg Hrvatskih Velikana 2. 023 383 123. www.tzg-biograd.hr

10 Lake Vrana

Situated just outside Biograd Na Moru, the largest lake in Croatia is over 13 km (8 miles) long. It is connected to the Adriatic via a system of underground channels and is home to numerous bird species. ◈ Map B4

Around Northern Dalmatia

Ask at Šibenik's Civic Museum (Gradska Vrata 3. 022 213 800) about visiting the Fort of St Nicholas and St John's Fortress.

Left **Pag** Middle **Pašman** Right **Ugljan**

Islands

Kornati Islands
This stunning necklace of unspoilt islands is a paradise for sailors and day-trippers. For the ultimate escape from it all, head for a deserted island for a taste of "Robinson Crusoe tourism" *(see pp26–7)*.

Murter
The gateway to the Kornati National Park is an island connected to the mainland by a bridge. As the main population centre, it is the place to come for supplies *(see p26)*. ⊗ Map B4

Pag
Famed for its eponymous sheep's cheese and the quality of its lamb, Pag is a notoriously dry island. Its unforgettable terrain looks like a moonscape and is unlike anywhere else in the Mediterranean. Pag Town also boasts an interesting old town *(see p37)*. ⊗ Map A2

Dugi Otok
Not actually within the Kornati National Park (as some tour operators may tell you), Dugi Otok is nevertheless a lovely place to spend the day, or to anchor a yacht for an afternoon. ⊗ Map A3

Pašman
Connected by a bridge to Ugljan, this island is home to a couple of modest fishing villages and a Benedictine monastery. There are ferry connections to Biograd Na Moru. ⊗ Map B3

Ugljan
The most heavily populated Adriatic island is popular with commuters from Zadar *(see pp30–31)*. Despite this, it retains something of an unspoilt feel, as well as producing some of the country's finest olive oil. ⊗ Map A3 • Tourist office: 023 288 011. www.ugljan.hr

Silba
Tree-cloaked Silba has a lived-in feel, unlike that of the many barren north Dalmatian islands, as it once stood on key trading routes. ⊗ Map A2 • Tourist office: 023 370 175

Zlarin
Visitors to this island can wander around the quiet village of Zlarin after the scenic ferry ride from Šibenik. This is a good place to pick up coral souvenirs before heading back to the mainland. ⊗ Map C4

Privič
The island neighbouring Zlarin is the setting for a clutch of attractive villages, an old church with Baroque altarpieces and a decent beach. ⊗ Map C4

Iž
This island is a favourite unspoilt escape for the citizens of Zadar, from which there is a direct ferry. There is little to do here apart from having an amble around the olive groves and a swim in the sea. ⊗ Map A3

Ask at the tourist office in Šibenik for more information about Zlarin, Iž and Privič, and in Biograd Na Moru for details on Pašman.

Left **Sunset strip, Šibenik** Middle **Aurora, Primošten** Right **Maya Pub, Zadar**

🔟 Cafés, Bars and Nightlife

1 Sunset Strip, Šibenik
Relax with a drink by the water's edge in Šibenik old town. Here you can enjoy the sunset at one of the sprinkling of outdoor cafés, as their sound systems vie with each other. ◈ *Map C4*

2 No.4 Club, Šibenik
This city-centre bar specializes in great cocktails – beware, though, as they tend to be on the strong side. Food is on offer too, and there is a terrace. ◈ *Trg Dinka Zavorovicar 4 • Map C4*

3 Zrće, Novalja, Pag
Although the "Croatian Ibiza" is not on the same scale as the Spanish original, this is a popular party beach. It has three big night-clubs, and many bars and fast-food outlets, all of which help fuel the summer fun. ◈ *Map A2*

4 Saloon, Pag Town, Pag
The former salt warehouse across the bridge from Pag's old town is transformed into a buzzing nightclub in the summer months. It opens its doors nightly during July and August and every Friday and Saturday in June and September. ◈ *Map A2*

5 Caffè Bar Forum, Zadar
Soak up the view of the Roman remains and spectacular ecclesiastical buildings that can be seen from this friendly café. Outdoor tables spread right out into the Roman forum in summer. ◈ *Široka 24 • Map B3*

6 Gotham, Zadar
This fun-filled nightlife complex, located to the north of Zadar's old town, boasts a club/café and cinema. Renovated in 2005, it has a Batman theme. ◈ *Marka Oreškovića 1 • Map B3*

7 Maya Pub, Zadar
A Balinese decor and lounge sounds are the order of the day in this bright and popular space. Expect surroundings decked out with exotic sculptures and a suitably chilled-out clientele. ◈ *Liburnska Obala 6 • Map B3*

8 The Garden, Zadar
This new arrival, owned by British reggae band UB40's drummer James Brown and Nick Colgan, is the place to see and be seen in Zadar. ◈ *Bedemi Zadarskih Pobuna • Map B3*

9 Aurora, Primošten
There are three dance floors, a chill-out room, restaurants and even a swimming pool at this huge out-of-town nightclub complex. Big DJ names to have featured here recently include Roger Sanchez and David Morales. ◈ *Kamenar bb • Map C4*

10 Club Hacienda, Vodice
The open-air Hacienda Club is a big venue in an equally large resort. It has boasted inter-national names such as Benny Benassi and the Shapeshifters and releases its own compilation CDs. ◈ *Magistrala bb • Map C4*

In Croatian addresses, "bb" is short for bez broj, meaning "without number."

Foša, Zadar

⁝⁝10 Places to Eat

Konoba Branimir, Nin
Simple Dalmatian cuisine, a cosy atmosphere and a small terrace overlooking the oldest church in Croatia make this rustic eatery a fine choice. ⊗ *Višeslavov Trg 2 • Map B3 • 023 264 866 • KK*

Restaurant Perin Dvor, Nin
At this friendly restaurant, close to Nin's Donji Most (Lower Bridge), you can dine on fresh fish and simple Dalmatian grills on an attractive garden terrace. The town's majorettes cause a stir from time to time by practising outside. ⊗ *Hrvatskog Sabora 1 • Map B3 • 023 264 307 • KKK*

Konoba "85", Novalja
Set back from Novalja's busy Riva and open year round, this restaurant serves up first-rate fish dishes and is frequented by locals. The creamy tagliatelle with prawns is a must. ⊗ *Josipa Kunkere 4 • Map A2 • 053 663 680 • KKK*

Zlatna Ribica, Brodarica
On Friday and Saturday evenings, live piano music fills this upmarket fish restaurant *(see p48)*, which has an adjoining pension. ⊗ *Krapanjskih Spuzvara 46 • Map C4 • 022 350 300 • KKKK*

Foša, Zadar
Fresh fish, and an unbeatable location just outside Zadar's Land Gate, ensure that this local favourite is always busy *(see p48)*. ⊗ *Kralja Dmitra Zvonimira 2 • Map B3 • 023 314 421 • KKKK*

Kornat, Zadar
Kornat's friendly waiting staff serve up innovative meat and fish dishes in elegant surrounds. Non-smokers note: smoking is permitted throughout. ⊗ *Liburnska Obala 6 • Map B3 • 023 254 501 • KKK*

Gradska Vjećnica, Šibenik
Most people come here for the view as much as the food. Dine on shellfish, delicate white fish or grilled meat in the shadow of the Cathedral of St James *(see pp28–9)*. ⊗ *Trg Republike Hrvatske 1 • Map C4 • 022 213 065 • KKK*

Tamaris, Dugi Otok
This simple *konoba* (inn) serves grilled meat, and fish straight from the Adriatic. ⊗ *Obala Kralja Tomislava, Sali • Map B3 • 023 377 236 • Closed Nov–Mar • KK*

Hotel Restaurant Biser, Pag Town, Pag
The menu at this award-winning restaurant includes local delicacies such as spit-roast Pag lamb, salty *Paški sir* and *pršut (see p48)*. Booking essential in high season. ⊗ *Antuna Gustava Matoša 8 • Map A2 • 023 611 333 • KKKKK*

Restoran Dalmacija, Primošten
This old-town restaurant serves innovative Dalmatian cuisine, with dishes like octopus with pineapple and tuna *carpaccio* alongside more simple meat dishes and grills. ⊗ *Put Murve 15 • Map C4 • 022 570 009 • Closed Nov–Mar • KKK*

For more restaurant listings **See pp48–9, 68, 69, 87, 97**

Left **The fish market, housed in a 16th-century loggia, Trogir Old Town** Right **Gradac**

Central Dalmatia

ENTRAL DALMATIA HAS IT ALL – *a large, vibrant city with a Mediterranean swagger, a wealth of historic towns, and some of the country's most popular islands. The city in question, Split, is Croatia's second biggest, after Zagreb. It's also the nation's busiest ferry hub, making it a great base for exploring the likes of lavender-infused Hvar, Brač, famous for the marble which helped build the White House, and remote Vis, many Croats' favourite Adriatic island. Traces of the various civilizations that have swept through the region emerge colourfully, with epic Roman remnants like Diocletian's Palace in Split and the ruined town of Salona, while the Venetian empire too has left its mark, on Trogir, Hvar and Vis. With an increasing number of flights into Split, and the brand new motorway linking it to Zagreb and the European road network, this scenically stunning corner of Croatia seems on an inexorable rise.*

TOP 10 Sights

1. Trogir Old Town
2. Diocletian's Palace, Split
3. Kaštela
4. Salona
5. Makarska Riviera
6. Gradac
7. Klis
8. Brela
9. Omiš
10. Živogošće and Zaostrog

Main Hall, Diocletian's Palace

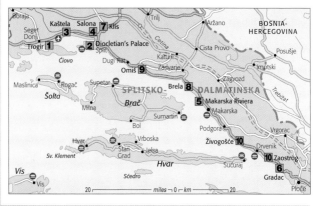

Trogir Old Town

When you've explored the profusion of churches, palaces and grand buildings that this perfectly preserved gem has to offer, relax on the wide waterfront Riva, where pavement cafés and al fresco restaurants bubble with activity day and night (see pp18–19).

Kaštel Lukšić

Diocletian's Palace, Split

Make sure to leave plenty of time to explore and relax in one of the most atmospheric city centres in Europe; the warren-like palace complex can be so captivating that day-trippers often end up missing their ferry, or just deciding to stay for an unplanned day or two. The palace is not at all what you expect an ancient monument to be like; it's full of life, with people hanging their washing out of the windows of flats set into its walls, bustling restaurants in lavish courtyards, and funky bars, where the local "beautiful people" (the Spličani are renowned for their beauty, and big model agencies regularly send scouts here) come to see and be seen (see pp22–3).

Kaštela

Between Split and Trogir, an untidy morass of cheap housing and light industry surrounds the main road, but by the coast, the hidden gems of Kaštela await discovery. The "castles" from which the area takes its name date back as far as the 15th century, when they were built both as coastal defences and lavish retreats for the local nobles; you can walk from one to the next along the coast. The highlights are Kaštel Stari (the oldest), which has a decent stretch of beach, pretty Kaštel Gomolica, Kaštel Kambelovac, which boasts a seafood restaurant, and Kaštel Lukšić, which has been converted into a modest gallery and café.
🅢 Map D5 • Tourist info: Brce 1, Dvorac Vitturi, Kaštel Lukšić. 021 228 355

Salona

Salona (the name derives from the Latin word for salt) is the supposed birthplace of Emperor Diocletian (see p25). Nowadays it's just a ruin, with none of the life and energy of Diocletian's Palace, but this old Roman town just outside Split does allow visitors to gain an insight into ancient Roman life. If you can forget the stranglehold of the surrounding industrial development, it's a pretty site, with mountains to one side and the Adriatic to the other. The Tusculum is a good place to begin your exploration. Also look out for the amphitheatre, the Roman baths, the old Forum, the Theatre and the Necropolis of Manastirine. 🅢 Map D5

Necropolis of Manastirine, Salona

Head to the second floor of Diocletian's Palace to escape the summer crowds.

81

Franciscan monastery, Makarska Riviera

Makarska Riviera

5 A mecca for Bosnians and citizens of the former Soviet bloc countries, this massively popular coastal strip south of Split is not to everyone's taste. Still, if you can find a quiet stretch of beach, then it can be a pleasant place to sit, gazing out at the islands of Brač and Hvar from the shade of the pine trees that fringe it. The resort of Makarska has some interesting old buildings and a lively bustle of bars, cafés and restaurants. ⊗ Map F5 • Tourist info: Obala Kralja Tomislava 16. 021 612 002. www.makarska.hr

Gradac

6 Gradac is best known for its beach, which at 6 km (4 miles) is the longest on the Croatian coast. It's a spectacular spot, with the Biokovo Mountains rising to the north and the islands of Central Dalmatia to the south. There's plenty of shade to keep the worst ravages of the summer sun at bay, as well as a flurry of campsites and hotels for those who fancy an extended stay (see p43). ⊗ Map J1 • Tourist info: Stjepana Radića 1. 021 697 375. www.gradac.hr

Klis

7 This hulking fortress complex in the mountains above Split enjoys a stunning setting, with impressive views of the city, mountains, sea and islands. The Romans were the first to use the site. Later it became a bulwark against the Ottomans, who finally captured it in 1513 after a bitter siege; they held it for more than a century, to the dismay of the residents of Split. Today, Klis is justifiably famed for a trio of roadside restaurants specializing in spit-roasted lamb. ⊗ Map D5 • Tourist info: Megdan 57. 021 240 578. www.tzo-klis.hr

The Fortress of Klis

Language and Nationhood

Under French rule (1806–13), Croatian became the "official" language of Dalmatia, but when the Austrians took over in 1813, they re-introduced Italian as the language of public life – an important spur for the growth of Croatian nationalism. In 1865, Makarska became one of the first communes to bring back Croatian as its official language.

Brela

8 Travelling south from Split, this is the first resort you come to on the Makarska Riviera, and one of the nicest spots to while away a day or two just relaxing by the sea. Brela is a pleasant town with a gaggle of old stone houses and a few modern hotels and restaurants, but it's the beach that people come for – a tree-shrouded sinew of pebble and shingle that curls around the coast north of the town. ⊗ Map E5 • Tourist info: Trg A. Stepinca bb. 021 618 455. www.brela.hr

In Croatian addresses, "bb" is short for bez broj, meaning "without number".

Omiš

Set at the point where the Cetina river emerges from its rugged gorge to discharge into the Adriatic, Omiš is a good base for rafting trips *(see p44)*, and a convenient jumping-off point for the gorge and its enjoyable fish restaurants. Once a notorious pirate bolthole, these days Omiš is a largely modern town, although it does have a small historic quarter, and there are some atmospheric old fortifications in the hills above the town. ◈ *Map E5 • Tourist info: Trg Kneza Miroslava bb. 021 861 350. www.tz-omis.hr*

Živogošće and Zaostrog

At the southern end of the Makarska Riviera is the small resort of Živogošće. The oldest settlement on this stretch of the coastline, it is home to a 17th-century Franciscan monastery with an impressive Baroque altar and a renowned library whose holdings shed light on life during the Ottoman occupation of the region. Slightly further south is Zaostrog, home to an older (16th-century) Franciscan monastery, an attractive site with a small art gallery and folk museum. ◈ *Map H1 • Tourist info: Živogošće bb. 021 605 069. www.zivogosce.hr*

Franciscan monastery, Zaostrog

Island-hopping

Morning

⏱ During high season, a number of companies operate hydrofoils that help the big Jadrolinija ferries *(see p103)* transport passengers around the central Dalmatian islands, making it possible to spend a long day island-hopping.

☕ Start the day with a light breakfast at one of the small quayside cafés near the ferry terminal in **Split** before heading out on the first Jadrolinija ferry to **Vis** *(see p84)*. After a stroll around Vis Town's water-front, head for the Venetian-style **Kut** district *(see p37)* in time for lunch at one of its excellent restaurants *(see pp48, 87)*. Head back to the ferry terminal and catch a fast ferry to **Hvar Town** *(see p36)*. If you've overindulged, you can work off lunch with a brisk hike up to the fortress above the town.

Afternoon

Time now for the last island of the day, so head by hydrofoil to the resort of **Bol** on the island of **Brač** *(see p84)*, home to Croatia's most famous beach, **Zlatni Rat** *(see p42)*. If the fancy takes you, you could relax and spend the night here. Otherwise, head back to Split – either from Bol, or from the port of Supetar on the other side of the island, where Jadrolinija ferries run till late.

Note: sailing schedules are liable to change as often as the unpredictable Adriatic winds, so this itinerary should be carefully planned. Check timetables at the ferry terminal in Split, or at the kiosks at the southern end of the Riva.

Left **Hvar** Middle **Vis** Right **Brač**

🔟 Islands

1 Biševo
This isle off Vis is home to the famed Blue Grotto, with its stunning visual play of water and light. Boat trips operate from Komiža. ◈ *Map C6 • Tourist office: Riva Sv Mikule 2, Komiža • 021 713 455*

2 Hvar
One of the sunniest Adriatic islands is cloaked by an aromatic blanket of lavender and other wild herbs. The highlight of this long, sinewy isle is Hvar Town *(see p36)*. ◈ *Map D6 • Tourist office: Trg Sveti Stjepana • 021 741 059 • www.tzhvar.hr*

3 Vis
Once an off-limits military base, this rugged and unspoilt island is popular with Croats and, increasingly, tourists too. Charming Vis Town lies across the hills from Komiža. ◈ *Map D6 • Tourist office: Šetalište Stare Isse 5, Vis Town • 021 717 017 • www.tz-vis.hr*

4 Brač
Marble from this mountainous island just off Split was used for Diocletian's Palace, the Hungarian Parliament and the White House in Washington DC. Brač also boasts Croatia's most famous beach, Zlatni Rat *(see p42)*. ◈ *Map E5 • Tourist office: Porat Bolskih Pomoraca bb, Bol • 021 635 638 • www.bol.hr*

5 Šolta
This often overlooked island, located right next to Split, is well worth a day trip, if not an overnight stay. ◈ *Map D5*

6 Pakleni Islands
The "Islands of Hell" are, contrary to what their name suggests, simple rustic places. They are great for getting away from the glitz and weight of history of Hvar Town and spending a day sunbathing and swimming *(see p42)*.

7 Drvenik Mali
"Small Drvenik" has a pleasant bay, where those looking to escape the heat of Trogir in summer can chill out for a while, but few facilities. ◈ *Map C5*

8 Drvenik Veli
"Big Drvenik" offers an agreeable town of the same name, which welcomes visiting yachts and has a couple of *pensions* and fish restaurants. Other parts of the island offer good swimming. ◈ *Map D5*

9 Čiovo
This island is joined by a bridge to Trogir *(see p81)*. The views back from Čiovo to Trogir's old town are worth the walk alone. There is a marina and also a sprinkling of places to eat and drink. ◈ *Map D5*

10 Šćedro
This sparsely populated island near Hvar offers some attractive beaches, as well as a ruined Roman villa in Rake Bay and the remains of a Dominican monastery in Mostir Bay. ◈ *Map G1*

Ferries link Split to Šolta, and Trogir to Drvenik Mali and Veli. Water taxis go to the Pakleni Islands and Šćedro from Hvar Town.

Cetina Gorge

Top10 Inland Excursions

1 Sinj
A historic mountain town with some interesting churches, on 15 August annually, Sinj hosts the massively popular Sinjska Alka medieval festival (which bears some similarities to Siena's famous *Palio*). ◈ *Map E4*
• *Tourist office: Vrlička 50 • 021 826 352*

2 Plitvice Lakes
The UNESCO World Heritage listed Plitvice Lakes are an oasis of limestone pools, lakes and waterfalls that lie within a well organized national park. ◈ *Map B1*
• *053 751 015 • www.np-plitvicka-jezera.hr • Open 8am–6pm daily • Adm charge*

3 Cetina Gorge
This starkly beautiful gorge cuts through the heart of Central Dalmatia, before a rendezvous with the Adriatic at Omiš. It is increasingly popular with rafters, who often start near the town of Penšići. Foodies savour its fish restaurants. ◈ *Map E4*

4 Gubavica Falls
Near the village of Zadvarje, to the north of Omiš, the Cetina river plunges dramatically almost 50 m (165 ft) through the karst landscape. ◈ *Map E5*

5 Zadvarje
This village is a good spot for appreciating the beauty of the Cetina Gorge. From the cliffs around here the waterfalls look particularly impressive after heavy rain. ◈ *Map E5*

6 Mosor
A mountain range extending between Klis and Omiš, Mosor attractively frames the Cetina river and a number of small villages. Explore it by car, or join the Croatian climbers tackling the barren Mosor Mountain. ◈ *Map E5*

7 Red Lake (Crveno Jezero)
You cannot see this 300-m (1,000-ft) wide lake near Imotski from afar, as it lies tucked away in an inaccessible pit. The strange ochre hue its waters take on comes from the surrounding landscape. ◈ *Map F5*

8 Blue Lake (Modro Jezero)
It is possible to get down to water level at this pit lake, which takes on a contrasting colour to its sibling, the Red Lake. In summer, low waters reveal bizarre rock formations at this spooky place. ◈ *Map F5*

9 Mostar
This Bosnian city has a famous bridge linking its two sides, over the Neretva river *(see p67)*. ◈ *off map • Tourist office: 387 (0)36 580 275*

10 Livno
A southern Bosnian town, just across the Croatian border, Livno is renowned for its tasty cheese, which is very inexpensive to buy here, though be aware that it is unpasteurized. ◈ *Map E4 • www.bhtourism.ba*

Visitors to Croatia from Europe, the USA, Australia and New Zealand do not currently need visas to enter Bosnia or Montenegro.

85

Bačvice, Split

🔟 Cafés, Bars and Nightlife

Vidilica, Split
Sweeping views of the city and its busy port are to be had from this café on the Marjan hillside. It is worth the hike up on a sunny day just to sit back with a cold drink and take in the scene. ◈ *Nazorov Prilaz 1 • Map P5*

Puls 2, Split
This perennially popular bar has a great location at the heart of Diocletian's Palace. In summer there are cute low outdoor tables and chairs. Loud music fills the dark interior. ◈ *Buvinina 1 • Map P2*

Bačvice, Split
Located south of the centre of Split, this massively popular modern nightlife complex is set on the bay of the same name. There's a multitude of bars, cafés, restaurants and nightclubs to choose from. Great fun on a hot summer evening. ◈ *Map Q6*

Ghetto Club, Split
This retreat of the local cognoscenti gets few tourists as it is on the often-ignored upper level of the Diocletian's Palace. It has a busy bar and a spacious courtyard for summer use.
◈ *Dosud 10 • Map P2*

F1, Trogir
This big and highly popular dance-music orientated nightclub draws in the crowds from Trogir, 5 km (3 miles) away, and Split, 20 km (12 miles) away. ◈ *Junction of Magistrala and airport road • Map D5*

Smokvica, Trogir
This café-bar in the shadow of the cathedral opens at 7am for *espresso* and keeps going till the small hours, by which time it has metamorphosed into a buzzing live-music venue with an extensive cocktail menu.
◈ *Radovanov Trg 9 • Map D5*

Art Café, Makarska
It would be worth coming to Makarska just to visit this bar – a chic and classy place that spills out into an attractive courtyard.
◈ *Don Mihovila Pavlinovića 1 • Map F5*

Venerada, Hvar Town
This summer venue has an open-air cinema and various club nights. It is located on the hill behind the Delfin Hotel. Keep your eyes peeled for adverts for it around town. ◈ *Map D6*

Carpe Diem, Hvar Town
Hvar Town boasts this ultra-cool Ibiza-style cocktail bar that pumps out mellow tunes through to the early hours of the morning. Watch from the summer terrace as yachts cruise in and out of the harbour. ◈ *Riva bb • Map D6*

Faces Club, Bol, Brač
Near the resort of Bol, one of the best beaches in Croatia *(see p42)* is complemented by one of the country's largest outdoor discos. This is what happens when Split's trendy Masters Club branches out onto the island of Brač. ◈ *Map E5*

Recommend your favourite bar on traveldk.com

Price Categories

For a three course	**K** under 100kn
meal for one with half	**KK** 100–150kn
a bottle of wine (or	**KKK** 150–200kn
equivalent meal), taxes	**KKKK** 200–250kn
and extra charges.	**KKKKK** over 250kn

Nostromo, Split

🔟 Places to Eat

1 Stellon, Split
A funky favourite with 20- and 30-somethings out at Bačvice, Stellon offers delicious seafood, meat dishes and pizzas, tempting drinks, and wonderful sea views *(see p48)*. ✆ Bačvice bb • Map Q6 • 021 347 932 • KK

2 Nostromo, Split
Right by the fish market is this trim seafood restaurant. Sit upstairs and you can watch as the ultra-fresh seafood for your platter is grilled *(see p48)*. ✆ Kraj Sv Marije 10 • Map N2 • 091 505 6666 • KKKK

3 Šumica, Split
A favourite with besuited business types, this classy joint is set in woodland near the Adriatic. It produces both meat and seafood dishes, with panache. There is an outdoor terrace. ✆ Put Firula 6 • Map Q6 • 021 389 897 • KKKK

4 Restoran Fontana, Trogir
Trogir old town's best hotel has a great restaurant with a terrace where diners can absorb the atmosphere of the Riva *(see p49)*. Unlike many places in town, it is open all year. ✆ Obrovo 1 • Map D5 • 021 884 811 • KKK

5 Restoran Monika, Trogir
Set within its own courtyard in Trogir's old town, Monika is an atmospheric dining choice. Grilled seafood is the speciality, and the place is packed out in high season. ✆ Budislaviceva 12 • Map D5 • 021 884 808 • Closed late Dec–Mar • KKK

6 Macondo, Hvar Town
This top-quality seafood restaurant in Hvar's old town is no longer a local secret – so book ahead. Prices are suitably steep. In summer you can eat outside. ✆ Groda bb • Map D6 • 021 742 850 • KKKK

7 Palača Paladini, Hvar Town
Tuck into delicious grilled fish and meat dishes in a courtyard full of orange trees. Smooth service and good vegetarian food are other plus points. ✆ Petra Hektorovića 4 • Map D6 • 021 742 104 • KKK

8 Vila Kaliopa, Vis Town
A treat is in store for diners at this simply divine restaurant. Top-notch seafood is served in a sculpture-laden garden in the Kut district of Vis Town *(see p48)*. ✆ Nazora 32 • Map D6 • 091 271 1755 • Closed Nov–Feb • KKKKK

9 Restoran Pojoda, Vis Town
This upmarket restaurant, with an ornate courtyard, charges by the kilo for top-class fish. The fine food comes with a wine list and service to match. ✆ Don Cvjetka Marasovića 8 • Map D6 • 021 711 575 • KKKKK

10 Taverna, Bol, Brač
You will find this friendly waterfront restaurant between the old town and Zlatni Rat beach, near where the fast ferries come in. Dalmatian specialities. ✆ Radica Frane 5 (Riva) • Map E5 • 021 635 236 • Closed Nov–Dec • KK

➤ *For more restaurant listings See pp48–9, 68, 69, 79, 97*

Left **Peljeŝac vineyards** Right **Konavle**

Southern Dalmatia

ESPITE THE POPULARITY of its most famous city, Dubrovnik, Southern Dalmatia remains relatively unexplored – and perhaps for that reason, unspoilt. Much of its appeal lies in the great diversity of the natural landscape, with pristine beaches, sheer cliffs, fertile farmland, dense forests, rolling hills and dramatic mountains all packed into a narrow and easily navigable strip of land. The Adriatic is never far away – generous provider of the top-quality seafood which can be served in even the most humble konoba (taverna), where you may also sample one of the excellent local wines from the vineyards of the Peljeŝac Peninsula. And when you think you've seen it all, it's easy to launch off into neighbouring Bosnia-Herzegovina or Montenegro.

Sights

Pebble beach, Orebić

Preceding pages **Belltower of the Franciscan monastery, Dubrovnik, seen through the colonnade of the Romanesque cloisters**

Neretva Delta

On its journey to the sea, the Neretva river fans out to create the lush, water-drenched landscape of the Neretva Delta. This 200-sq-km (77-sq-mile) expanse is partially navigable by boat, and can also be explored by car. Not only is the delta vital to Croatian agriculture, it provides a sanctuary for the myriad species of bird that stop off here as they migrate south to Africa. Many fish inhabit this angler's paradise, including eels and an indigenous species of trout. The Atlas Travel Agency organize visits from Dubrovnik. ⊗ Map J1 • Atlas Travel Agency: 0800 442 222. www.atlas-croatia.com

Orebić

This small seaside town on the Pelješac Peninsula has been quietly luring visitors for decades, with its idyllic location, long, sun-drenched pebble beaches, laid-back cafés and high-quality restaurants. Recently, Orebić has undergone something of a transformation, with luxurious apartments springing up as an alternative to the resort hotels nearby, and real-estate agents moving in to snare those tempted to stay. ⊗ Map H1 • Tourist info: Trg Mimbelli bb. 020 713 718. www.tz-orebic.com

Korčula Town

The historic core of Korčula Town is one of Dalmatia's most dramatic set-pieces. For the visitor, it offers attractive architecture, fine restaurants and tranquil waterside cafés from which to admire dazzling sunsets. The town is also something of an activity centre, with wind-surfing, yachting and diving all popular watersports (see pp16–17).

Korčula Town

Pelješac Vineyards

Many people treat the Pelješac Peninsula as little more than a quick route from Dubrovnik to Korčula Town. In doing so, they miss an opportunity to explore the vineyards that produce what is arguably Croatia's best red wine, Dingač. A guided tour is a simple way of rectifying this oversight; Atlas's Dubrovnik-based excursion takes in three cellars in the villages of Potomje and Prizdrina. From Potomje, tunnels bored into the Pelješac mountains lead to quiet beaches. ⊗ Map J2

14th-century fortifications, Ston

Ston

The Republic of Ragusa (see pp8–9) left an enduring reminder of its presence in Ston. The 14th-century fortifications, erected to guard against attack by sea, resemble a miniature Great Wall of China. Today's relaxed pace of life is a far cry from the days when Ston was the second most powerful centre in the Republic. Other attractions include salt pans, and stunning views of the Dinaric Mountains and the vaulting peaks of Bosnia. ⊗ Map J2 • Tourist info: Pelješki Put 1. 020 754 452. www.ston.hr

In Croatian addresses, "bb" is short for bez broj, meaning "without number".

91

Marco Polo

The island of Korčula is alleged by some to be the birthplace of legendary explorer Marco Polo – a claim hotly disputed by both Venice and Genoa. There is evidence to suggest that he at least visited Korčula Town, so the idea may not be total fantasy – something the locals have seized upon, with "Marco Polo's House" now open as a museum.

Mali Ston

A short walk north of Ston is its smaller sibling, Mali Ston. Gastronomes from all over Croatia and Italy flock to "Little Ston" to savour the finest fresh fish, with shellfish plucked straight from the Stonski Channel a highlight on any menu. The scenery is as spectacular as the seafood, and it is perhaps unsurprising that this idyllic waterside spot with its aphrodisiac oysters has become a popular haunt with amorous Croatian weekend-breakers. Some of the restaurants have rooms – which at least helps prevent arguments about who is going to drive. ◈ Map K2

Trsteno Arboretum

At the beginning of the 16th century, the Gučetić family sowed the seeds of what has since become one of Europe's most impressive arboretums. Making the most of its dramatic seaside setting, this expansive collection of trees and plants from around the world tumbles towards the Adriatic, with fine views of Trsteno harbour and the Elafiti Islands beyond. Highlights of this tranquil oasis 20 km (12 miles) northwest of Dubrovnik include a 500-year-old plane tree, a water garden whose ornate fountain depicts Neptune surrounded by nymphs, and an aqueduct. ◈ Potok 20, Trsteno • Map K2 • 020 751 019 • Open summer: 8am–7pm daily; winter: 8am–5pm daily • Adm charge

Fountain of Neptune, Trsteno Arboretum

Mljet National Park

The western corner of Mljet was designated a National Park in 1960, in a bid to conserve the island's holm oak and Aleppo pine forests. Among the main attractions are the interconnected saltwater lakes, Veliko Jezero ("Great Lake") and Malo Jezero ("Small Lake"). The former is home to the striking and frequently remodelled 12th-century Monastery of St Mary, which dominates the eponymous Sveta Marija Island. Another highlight is the small village of Polače, with its Roman ruins and dramatic setting astride Mljet's most attractive harbour. ◈ Pristanište 2, 20226 Goveđari • Map J2 • 020 744 041 • www.np-mljet.hr • Adm charge; children free

Mljet National Park

Cavtat

Croatia's most southerly resort was first settled in the 3rd century BC, and it still bears the marks of the Illyrians, Greeks, Romans and Slavs who occupied it at one time or another. When you're not sampling the café-life on the waterfront promenade, look out for the 16th-century Rector's Palace, and a mausoleum by Ivan Meštrović commissioned by the wealthy Račić family. Also worth a visit is the Vlaho Bukovac Gallery, dedicated to the memory of one of Croatia's most famous painters. ◈ Map L3 • Vlaho Bukovac Gallery: Vlahe Bukovca 5. 020 478 646. 10am–1pm, 4–8pm Tue–Sun. Adm charge

Vlaho Bukovac (1855–1922), self-portrait

Konavle

The dramatic landscape of this narrow strip of land extending from Cavtat down to Kotor Bay in Montenegro is characterized by harsh karst rock, verdant forests and sheer cliffs. An exploration of the area turns up ancient burial cairns, ruined fortresses, the remnants of a Roman aqueduct, and hills studded with vines and olive groves. Less obvious to casual visitors is the destruction wreaked during the war of the early 1990s, when many of the area's villages were decimated. Organized "safaris" are a good option (see p67). ◈ Map L3

A Drive Along the Pelješac Peninsula

Morning

Forty-five minutes north of Dubrovnik on the Adriatic Highway (a scenic though frustrating drive), a sign-posted left turn leads onto the mountainous Pelješac Peninsula; the town of **Mali Ston** is a short distance further on. Time your arrival for a first-class early lunch of oysters and fresh fish in the wonderful Vila Koruna (see p48). After lunch, make the short journey to Mali Ston's sibling, **Ston**, and explore its rugged old walls (currently being considered for inclusion on UNESCO's World Heritage list). Back in the car, follow the main road as it heads inland, emerging after half an hour or so by the **Malo More** ("Small Sea") on the northeast coast of the peninsula. Make a brief pit-stop at the Beach Bar (see p96), with its great waterside location.

Afternoon

Back on the main road, **Janjina** (see p94), a little further on, is a good place to pull up and buy home-produced wine; just look out for signs. Alternatively, continue on the same route until you reach **Potomje**, the home of Croatia's best red wine, Dingač. Some of the cellars here welcome visitors (but remember that Croatian law prohibits drivers from consuming any alcohol). Continue northwest to the low-key resort of **Orebić**, whose beaches and scenic location merit an overnight stay; or take a car ferry across the Pelješki Kanal to **Korčula Town** (see pp16–17) and spend the night there. If you have to get back to Dubrovnik, it's only a two-hour drive away.

Left **Bust of Roman emperor Vespasian at Vid's museum** Right **Janjina**

Best of the Rest

1 Viganj
This small settlement with a 17th-century Dominican monastery unfolds around the Bay of Viganj, backed by the Pelješac mountains and looking out to the island of Korčula. Windsurfers flock to this picturesque spot for its windswept beaches. ◈ *Map H1*

2 Vid
Inhabited by both Greeks and Romans, Vid thrived as a trading post between the islands and the hinterland until the 7th century AD. View the remains of Roman Narona around the town and at Vid's museum. ◈ *Map J1*

3 Čilipi
With regular folk events and an ethnographic museum, Čilipi is on the tour circuit from Dubrovnik. On Sundays during high season the presence of performers in traditional costumes brightens up the main square. ◈ *Map L3*

4 Orašac
This pleasant village 15 km (9 miles) north of Dubrovnik has a fine 15th-century church and a palatial 16th-century villa. Its small marina and decent beach face the Elafiti Islands. ◈ *Map K2*

5 Lumbarda
Located to the east of Korčula Town, this pretty settlement lures visitors with its sandy beaches *(see p43)* and secluded coves, as well as the water sports on offer in summer. ◈ *Map H2*

6 Baćina Lakes
These six interlinked freshwater lakes just north of Ploče are an impressive sight. Surrounded by lush vegetation, they provide a habitat for a plethora of fish and bird species. ◈ *Map J1*

7 Kula Norinska
Dating from the 16th century, this seven-storey cylindrical tower at the junction of the Norin and Neretva rivers has formerly served as both a military lookout and a windmill. ◈ *Map J1*

8 Trpanj
The Pelješac Peninsula's north coast is the picturesque setting for a small resort with a pebble beach and a cluster of pavement cafés. Trpanj affords sweeping views across Malo More towards the hulking Biokovo Mountains. ◈ *Map H1*
• *Tourist office: Žalo 7* • *020 743 433*

9 Trstenik
On the west coast of the Pelješac Peninsula you can visit relaxed Trstenik, with old stone houses and a sheltered harbour. Protected by the hills that rear up behind it, the village has seaward views of Mljet and Lastovo. ◈ *Map J2*

10 Janjina
This compact village, with an ornate church, tumbles down the Pelješac hillside towards the sea. It's a great place to pick up wine from local vineyards. ◈ *Map J2*

The Dubrovnik-Neretva Country Tourist Board can provide more details on these sights: Cvijete Zuzorić 1/l, Dubrovnik, 020 323 887.

Left **Badija** Right **Koločep**

TOP 10 Islands

1 Lokrum
The most southerly of the Elfati Islands, this tree-shrouded, beach-fringed nature reserve is a perfect day-trip from Dubrovnik. It is home to the Natural History Museum, set in the cloister of a ruined 10th-century Benedictine monastery. ◈ Map L3

2 Koločep
One of the Elafiti Islands, Koločep's main attraction is a sandy beach that is seldom as crowded as Dubrovnik's, a short ferry ride away. There are two small villages to explore, as well as the dense woods that cover most of the island. ◈ Map K2

3 Lopud
Once a populous stronghold of the Republic of Ragusa, Lopud now enjoys a peaceful retirement. An old monastery, churches and a choice of beaches make this Elafiti island worth a visit. ◈ Map K2

4 Šipan
There is little to do bar relax and take in the rays on this quiet Elafiti retreat. It has a hotel and a couple of pensions. ◈ Map K2

5 Lastovo
A remote and little-developed island, Lastovo is a relaxed place where you can escape the tourist throngs. Lastovo Town is unusual in that it turns its back on the sea. ◈ Map G2 • Tourist office: Lastovo bb, Lastovo Town • 020 801 018 • www.lastovo-tz.net

6 Sušac
A tiny island near Lastovo, Sušac is accessible by private boat. Its 19th-century lighthouse, which offers inspirational views, can be rented out (see p115). Snorkelling and scuba diving options are good. ◈ Map K2

7 Korčula
Perhaps the most interesting of the southern Dalmatian islands boasts the gem of Korčula Town (see pp16–17), vineyards and beaches. ◈ Map H1

8 Badija
Just off Korčula – and reached by taxi boat – is this small island, once home to a community of Franciscan monks. The Franciscan church and monastery are both well preserved and make a striking sight by the sea. ◈ Map H1

9 Majsan
Even smaller than Badija is Majsan, which is also reached by taxi boat from Korčula Town. The relics on this island include the remains of a Roman settlement and the ruined medieval church of St Maximus. ◈ Map H1

10 Palagruža
This slip of land extends out into the Adriatic to the very edge of Croatian territorial waters. The 100-m (330-ft) tall lighthouse, offering Robinson Crusoe breaks (see p115), is a rare feature on an island that has to be reached by private boat. ◈ off map

Tour boats leave Dubrovnik for Lokrum, Korčula and the Elafiti Islands, and Split for Lastovo and Korčula.

Left **Massimo, Korčula Town** Middle **Konoba Marko Polo, Korčula** Right **Waterfront, Orebić**

Cafés, Bars & Nightlife

1 Beach Café, near Lumbarda

The sandy beach of Pržina, south of Lumbarda, has a modest café-bar that makes a perfect spot to relax in between dips in the Adriatic, which tempts nearby. ◈ *Map H2*

2 Mamilo, Lastovo Town

You will find Lastovo Town's only year-round café-bar on a hill just behind the town. The friendly owner usually keeps it open until his last customer leaves. ◈ *Map G2*

3 Riva, Cavtat

While away a pleasant hour or so at one of the café-bars on Cavtat's waterfront, taking in the distinctly Mediterranean ambience and the views over the bay and offshore islands. ◈ *Map L3*

4 Massimo, Korčula Town

Perched atop one of the town's defensive bastions, this popular summer bar comes complete with a unique pulley system for drinks. You can appreciate the sunset, as the swallows swirl on the skyline. Food is served downstairs. ◈ *Šetalište Petra Kanavelića bb • Map H1*

5 Fresh, Korčula Town

The old part of Korčula Town can be pretty quiet late at night, but this is one of the livelier bars. Located by the bus station, it attracts local teenagers and visitors looking for some late-night action outside their hotels. ◈ *Šetalište Frana Kršinića bb • Map H1*

6 Hotel Korčula, Korčula Town

This terrace café overlooking Korčula Town's old port is a great place to enjoy a coffee while you take in the passing scene. ◈ *Obala bb (west harbour) • Map H1*

7 Konoba Marko Polo, Korčula Town

With tables at the edge of the old town, from which views of the mountains and the Pelješki Channel open up, this is a superb haunt. It is a restaurant, but you can drift in for a few drinks. ◈ *Šetalište Petra Kanavelića bb • Map H1*

8 Bella Vista, Pelješac Peninsula

All the buses between Dubrovnik and Korčula call here for a rest stop – and, if driving, you should too. Swathes of the Pelješac Peninsula can be admired from the terrace. ◈ *Sveti Križa 104 • Map J2*

9 Beach Bar, Pelješac Peninsula

This slightly kitsch beach bar, with palm trees, a thatched roof and gaudy signs, is a good place to stop for a cool drink as you traverse the Pelješac Peninsula. It is located between Drače and Janjina *(see p94)*. ◈ *Map J2*

10 Waterfront, Orebić

After a day relaxing on one of Dalmatia's best beaches *(see p42)*, unwind further in one of Orebić's waterfront cafés, with great views of Korčula. ◈ *Map H1*

In Croatian addresses, "bb" is short for bez broj, meaning "without number".

Kolona, Cavtat

🔟 Restaurants

1 Vila Koruna, Mali Ston
Arguably the best choice in a small town that boasts a number of first-class fish restaurants, Vila Koruna is a must for seafood lovers – and lovers in general *(see pp48, 113)*. ❧ Pelješkiput 1 • Map K2 • 020 754 999 • KK

2 Kapetanova Kuća, Mali Ston
Another popular Mali Ston eatery, Kapetanova Kuća serves up mussels plucked straight from the Malostonski Channel, fish grills and Pelješac wine. The squid-ink risotto is divine. ❧ Obala Marsala Tita 9 • Map K2 • 020 754 264 • KKKK

3 Adio Mare, Korčula Town
This popular seafood restaurant in the old town is a lively place to eat on a summer night. Grilled fish is the speciality *(see p48)*. ❧ Svetog Roka 2 • Map H1 • 020 711 253 • Closed lunch, Nov–Apr • KKK

4 Amfora, Orebić
This waterfront restaurant serves good-value Dalmatian food: huge plates of risotto, fish and shellfish, as well as Balkan grills like *čevapčići* (spicy meatballs). ❧ Kneza Domagoja 6 • Map H1 • 020 713 779 • Closed Nov–Apr • KK

5 Mlinica Taverna, Orebić
This rustic restaurant set in a former mill has a Dalmatian menu. It fills up with tour groups in July and August, so try to visit at other times. ❧ Obala Pomorala bb • Map H1 • 020 713 886 • KK

6 Konoba Bačvara, Lastovo Town
Set in a traditional stone house at the heart of town, this cosy *konoba* (inn) serves fish and regional staples. ❧ Počivalo bb • Map G2 • 020 801 131 • Closed Jan–May • KK

7 Ogigija, Mljet
As you might expect, the emphasis at this pension and restaurant, with a large terrace looking out over the sea, is on fish. ❧ Polače 17 • Map J2 • 098 606 863 • Closed Oct–Apr • KKK

8 Kolona, Cavtat
Kolona charms with its raised sea-view terrace, grilled fish and attentive service. Innovative dishes, such as raw swordfish drizzled in lemon, have crept onto to a largely Dalmatian menu. ❧ Put Tihe 2 • Map L3 • 020 478 269 • Closed Nov–Apr • KKK

9 Orsan, Zaton
A short drive to the north out of Dubrovnik brings you to this excellent little restaurant. Savour quality fresh seafood right by the Adriatic on their terrace, which is something of a local favourite. ❧ Štikovica 43 • Map K2 • 020 891 267 • Closed Dec–Mar • KKKK

10 Konoba Zure, Lumbarda
This rustic, family-run *konoba* offers delicious seafood dishes – try the *brodetto* (Dalmatian fish stew), the stewed octopus and the shellfish risotto. ❧ Lumbarda 239 • Map H2 • 023 712 008 • KKK

 For more restaurant listings See pp48–9, 68, 69, 79, 87

STREETSMART

TOP 10 OF DUBROVNIK & THE DALMATIAN COAST

An outdoor religious event in Split

Top 10 General Information

Language
Croatian grammar is complex. The key to good pronunciation is to master the letter sounds, including the accented č, ć, ž, š, čž and đ *(see p126)*. Every letter is pronounced, and the emphasis is almost always on the first syllable. English, Italian and German are widely understood in Dalmatia, but you will find that any efforts to speak Croatian will be appreciated.

Electricity and Water
Croatia is on 220V/50 cycles and standard plugs are of the European two-pin, round-pronged type. Bottled mineral water has become fashionable in Dalmatia, but tap water is usually safe to drink. Dalmatians claim that the water from lakes and streams is clean and free of bacteria, but it is sensible to purify it.

Opening Hours
As a rule of thumb Dalmatians conduct business from 8am to 4pm Monday to Friday. Banks are, however, open from 7am to 7pm. Post offices serve customers from 7am to 7pm during the week and also from 7am to 1pm on Saturdays. Café-bars generally open daily at 7am and close at 11pm, although some keep later hours. Most restaurants also stay open until 11pm.

Time Differences
Croatia is in the Central European Time Zone, which operates on GMT plus one hour. For daylight saving, clocks are put back an hour at the end of March and forward an hour in late September. Croatia is one hour ahead of the UK, six to nine hours ahead of the USA and seven to nine hours behind Australia.

Tourist Radio
During the tourist season, Hrvatska Radio Televizija (HRT) broadcasts a limited radio news bulletin in English and German. HR2 has an hourly traffic bulletin, also in English and German. Check frequencies locally as they vary.

Further Reading
The following books are useful sources on Croatia's recent history: Marcus Tanner's *Croatia: A Nation Forged in War*, Slavenka Drakulić's *Balkan Express: Fragments from the Other Side of War* and Stipe Mesić's *The Demise of Yugoslavia: A Political Memoir*.

Government
Croatia has a multi-party parliamentary system, with separate legislative and executive functions. The country's first democratically elected president, Stjepan Mesić, is currently serving a second term in office; Prime Minister Ivo Sanader and the HDZ (Croatian Democratic Union) have been in power since 2003.

Economy
Agriculture, food production, manufacturing (textiles, timber, metal-working and electrical), chemical industries, shipping and tourism are all vital components of the Croatian economy. Recent years have seen considerable foreign investment, particularly in the field of construction, and Croatia has increased its exports to the West. One black cloud is a high level of unemployment (around 19%). Croatia is currently in negotiation to become a member of the European Union.

Religion
Recent surveys suggest that almost 90 per cent of Croats are Roman Catholic, just under 5 per cent are Serb Orthodox, and around 1 per cent are Muslim.

Society and Culture
Dalmatians are passionate about food and fashion and express forthright opinions. A strong national consciousness reveals itself in folkloric traditions, particularly in Čilipi *(see p94)* and Korčula Town *(see pp16–17)*. In this Catholic society there are some conservative attitudes to divorce and homosexuality.

Preceding pages **The Stradun, Dubrovnik**

Left **Tourist information office** Right **The beach, where many Croatians head on public holidays**

🔟 Planning Your Trip

1 Insurance

A travel insurance policy covering delays, cancellations, baggage loss or damage, illness, accidents and legal costs is essential. Terms and conditions vary between policies; winter sports options and expensive equipment often incur an extra premium.

2 When to Go

Dalmatia basks in an agreeable Mediterranean climate. Summers are hot and winters mild. Despite this idyllic weather, the bulk of the region's tourist facilities close from the end of October until late April. May and September are the optimum months for a visit; the weather is good, everything is open, but the summer crowds are absent.

3 What to Pack

If taking a prescription medication, check that you have a full supply and that you know the pharmaceutical (as opposed to the brand) name. In summer, pack sun lotion, sunglasses and insect repellent; in winter, a warm coat; and at any time of year, a waterproof.

4 Tourist Information

Advance information is available through the Croatian National Tourist Board's website and its offices abroad. Many Dalmatian towns, cities and villages have a tourist office, though these may be closed out of season.
⬥ *Croatian National Tourist Board: www.croatia.hr*

5 Passports and Visas

A valid passport or national identity card is required to enter Croatia. Visitors from Australia, New Zealand, Japan, North America, South America and European countries can usually stay in the country for up to 90 days without a visa. Visitors from Africa need a visa, and should seek advice from the Croatian Ministry of Foreign Affairs, or an embassy or consulate. ⬥ *Croatian Ministry of Foreign Affairs: www.mfa.hr*

6 Embassies and Consulates

The Croatian Ministry of Foreign Affairs' website *(see above)* gives a list of Croatian embassies and consulates overseas, and of foreign embassies and consulates on Croatian soil. Most of these are in Zagreb; the UK also has consulates in Split and Dubrovnik. ⬥ *Dubrovnik: Buničeva Poljana 3/1. Map J6. 020 324 597 • Split: Obala Hrvatskog Narodnog Preporoda 10/III. Map P2. 021 346 007*

7 Customs

Goods to the value of HRK3,000, 200 cigarettes, 2 litres of liqueur, 2 litres of wine, 1 litre of spirits and 60 ml of perfume (or 250 ml of *eau de toilette*) can be taken into Croatia. HRK15,000 can also be brought into or taken out of the country. Foreign currency is not restricted, but sums over HRK40,000 in value must be declared.

8 Public Holidays

1 Jan, Easter Sunday and Monday, 1 May, Corpus Christi (May/Jun), 22 Jun, 25 Jun, 5 Aug, 8 Oct, 1 Nov, and 25 and 26 Dec are public holidays in Dalmatia. Banks, shops and some restaurants close on these days. Local holidays are also observed.

9 Timetables and Transfers

Plan any journey by public transport carefully; staff at information desks are there to help. Ferry timetables, in particular, are subject to change, and reduced services from October to April. Buses to meet ferry passengers are often absent in winter; request that a local travel agency or hotel help arrange your transfers.

10 Advance Reservations

In summer, hotels of all grades fill up fast. Book as far ahead as possible for July and August. Buying tickets in advance is essential during festivals *(see pp54–5)*, and recommended for bus travel. Reservations for taking your car on a ferry can avoid long queues.

Plastic shoes are a good investment if you are intending to go swimming from rock outcrops (the domain of sea urchins).

101

Left **Disabled parking sign** Right **Group travel**

Special Concerns

Students
International student cards don't carry much weight in Croatia. A Hostelling International card gives discounts at the Dubrovnik and Zadar youth hostels *(see p116)*.
⊗ *Hostelling International: www.hihostels.com*

Disabled Travellers
In a region where the key tourist sights are hundreds of years old, Dalmatia's narrow streets and historic buildings are not easily accessible to those in wheelchairs. Only the most modern hotels and restaurants have facilities for the disabled. Anyone with mobility needs should contact the Croatian National Tourist Board *(see p101)* for advice when planning their trip.

Gay and Lesbian Travellers
Attitudes towards homosexuality are often far from enlightened. Dalmatia does not have a gay scene to speak of and any public displays of affection between same-sex couples may well affront local people, or solicit negative attention; the Gay Pride procession in Zagreb in 2002 saw an attack by extremists.

Lone Females
Although some men have chauvinist attitudes, lone female travellers will usually be treated with respect. Nonetheless, it is wise to take some basic precautions, such as not walking alone in the dark. Meetings with strangers should be in busy public places during the day.

Senior Citizens
Many seniors visit Dalmatia. They receive a warm welcome, but few discounts in high season. UK-based Saga Holidays have a large presence in Croatia, with some hotels even having areas reserved for their Saga guests. ⊗ *Saga Holidays: www.saga.co.uk*

Vegetarians
Meat and fish dominate menus, with vegetarian options often limited to simple salads, pasta starters, risottos (often mushroom), vegetable accompaniments and cheese. More choice is available to those who self-cater – or picnic at a local beauty spot. Most towns and villages have food markets and well-stocked supermarkets.

Group Travel
In July and August Dubrovnik can feel overcrowded with tour groups. The Croatian National Tourist Office *(see p101)* will provide lists of foreign travel operators specializing in group travel.

Travelling with Children
Children are welcome almost anywhere and under 12s often receive discounted entrance to attractions. Additional beds and cots can be added to hotel rooms for a small charge (book in advance). Public baby changing facilities are scarce, but disposable nappies and baby food are easy to come by.

Travelling with Pets
The UK's Pet Travel Scheme allows dogs and cats to travel to Croatia and re-enter the UK by air (Dubrovnik to London Gatwick with Britannia Airways). Pets must have been vaccinated against rabies and have tested negative 6 months later. They require a passport and have to be treated for ticks and tapeworm by a Croatian vet before returning home. Contact Defra for more details.
⊗ *Defra (UK): 08459 335 577. www.defra.gov.uk*

Working in Croatia
Croatia is not part of the EU and high levels of unemployment make it hard for non-Croatians to find jobs. Most foreign workers are employed by multinationals or work at a distance for home-based companies. Voluntary work is available through exchange programmes; embassies *(see p101)* and the Croatian Heritage Foundation are good sources of information.
⊗ *Croatian Heritage Foundation: www.matis.hr*

Left **Domestic ferry** Right **Sailing**

🔟 Getting to and Around Dalmatia

1 By Air
There are direct flights to Dalmatia from over 15 European countries, among them the UK, Germany, Italy, France and the Netherlands. Those from outside Europe transit through Zagreb or a European airport. ⬡ *Croatia Airlines: www.croatiaairlines.hr*

2 Airports
Dalmatia has three international airports, Split, Dubrovnik and Zadar. ⬡ *Split Airport: Map D5. 021 203 555. www.split-airport. hr • Dubrovnik Airport: Map L3. 020 773 377. www. airport-dubrovnik.hr • Zadar Airport: Map B3. 023 205 800. www.zadar-airport.hr*

3 By Boat
Jadrolinija car ferries operate between Italy and Dalmatia (Ancona–Split and Bari–Dubrovnik). Adriatica, SEM Marina and SNAV have passenger services between Ancona and Split. SNAV also runs an Ancona–Zadar route. SEM Marina and Azzura Line both link Bari and Dubrovnik. ⬡ *Jadrolinija: www.jadrolinija.hr • SEM Marina: www.sem-marina. hr • Adriatica: www. adriatica.it • SNAV: www. snav.com • Azzura Line: www.azzuraline.com*

4 By Road
Routes from Western Europe traverse Slovenia. Access from Central and Eastern Europe is via Hungary. The Hrvatski Autoklub and national automobile associations can advise on crossing borders by car. ⬡ *Hrvatski Autoklub: www.hak.hr*

5 Cruising
Dubrovnik is firmly on the Mediterranean cruise-ship circuit. The likes of Royal Caribbean regularly drop anchor here, as do smaller ships, on their way to or from Venice, Istria and Montenegro. ⬡ *Royal Caribbean: www. royalcaribbean.com • JEM Trade: www.croatia-istria. com • Cruise Adriatic: www.cruiseadriatic.com*

6 Sailing
Dalmatia is emerging as something of a Mecca for sailors. With numerous islands and islets, hidden coves, seemingly endless swathes of unspoiled and dramatic coastline, and relatively calm seas, it is easy to understand why *(see pp46–7)*.

7 Domestic Ferry Services
Jadrolinija runs an array of ferries to Dalmatia's islands, with the bulk departing from Split, Šibenik and Zadar. Tickets must be purchased prior to boarding, from ticket kiosks, Jadrolinija offices or ferry terminals. Foot passengers can usually just turn up, but advance reservations for vehicles are recommended in July and August. SEM Marina run catamaran services from Split.

8 Taxis and Buses
Taxis can be booked or hailed. Bus stops and stations display timetables for local and national bus services. Bus fares are reasonable, though there is a charge for each piece of luggage in the hold.

9 Car Rental
To hire a car you must be at least 21, have held a full licence for 2 years, and have a passport and credit card. National auto-mobile clubs can advise on whether you need an International Driving Permit (most people don't). Check terms and conditions carefully. Sixt is a reputable hire company. ⬡ *Sixt: 01 665 1599. www.sixt.com*

10 Rules of the Road
The Croatian speed limits are: 50 kmph (30 mph) in towns, 80 kmph (50 mph) outside towns, 100 kmph (60 mph) on highways and 130 kmph (80 mph) on motorways. It is compulsory to wear seat belts and to have your headlights on. Note that there is now a policy of zero tolerance towards drink-driving; it is illegal to have a blood-alcohol level in excess of 0 mg per 100 ml. It is illegal to talk on a mobile phone while driving. The police must be informed of road accidents, and hazard warning triangles must be used at breakdowns. (For emergency phone numbers, *see p104*).

Croatia Airlines shuttle buses run between the airports and the city centres, and may be used by passengers of other airlines as well.

Left **Hospital** Right **Croatian policeman**

Security and Health

1 Reciprocal Health Agreements

Most European countries, including the UK and Ireland, have reciprocal health agreements with Croatia. Those covered by these agreements can get free emergency medical care in Croatia, but will have to pay for other consultations and prescription charges. As Croatia is not in the EU, you do not need an EHIC.

2 Travel Insurance

It is unwise to rely on reciprocal health agreements. Comprehensive travel insurance *(see p101)* can save huge sums if you become ill or are involved in an accident.

3 Bites and Stings

Stray animals may have rabies and should not be petted. The spines of sea urchins on rocky shorelines can cause infection, but you can prevent problems by wearing shoes. Ticks found in forests between April and August can carry tick-borne encephalitis or Lyme disease; cover up and wear insect repellent. In summer, the region's mosquitoes may also give you nasty bites.

4 Sun Precautions

Sunstroke, sunburn or dehydration can spoil a holiday. You can protect yourself by wearing sunscreen with a high SPF and a sunhat, and by drinking plenty of water.

5 Health Centres and Hospitals

All Dalmatia's main towns and cities have either a health centre or a hospital where you will be able to see a doctor. The quality of care is parallel to that given in many Western European countries, with clean and well-equipped facilities and highly-trained staff.

6 Pharmacies

Centrally located pharmacies *(ljekarna)* are found in most cities, towns and resorts. In rural areas you may have to travel some way to locate one. Opening hours are usually from 8am to 8pm Monday to Friday and from 8am to 2pm on Saturdays. Pharmacists often speak English and for minor ailments they can suggest suitable non-prescription medicines.

7 Crime

Crime rates are lower in Croatia than in most European countries, with serious crimes against tourists particularly rare. Tourists do, however, fall prey to pickpockets. Take a sensible approach to your personal safety and that of your valuables. If you become the victim of a crime, contact the police immediately.

8 Vehicle Breakdown

Rental cars in Croatia usually have emergency breakdown cover. If you are planning to take your own car, contact your automobile association to check how you can arrange international breakdown cover.

9 Documentation

The Croatian police are entitled to ask you to produce an identity card or passport at any time. You must also show one of these forms of ID when checking into accommodation. When driving, you must have the correct documentation with you, including your driver's licence, in case the police want to inspect it. Tourists are rarely stopped, but you can be fined for failing to produce documents.

10 Landmines

Most of Dalmatia has for years been clear of landmines laid in the war of the early 1990s, but they do still exist. Around Skradin, Krka National Park and the border area with Bosnia, fields and even whole villages still have signs warning of landmines. Walkers heading off the beaten track should use a recent map, stick to trails and seek local advice about the possibility of mines.

Emergency Phone Numbers

Police 92
Fire 93
Ambulance 94
Breakdown: 987
Maritime rescue: 9155

English is widely spoken in Croatia, as are German and Italian.

Left **ATM** Middle **Internet café** Right **Post office**

🔟 Banking and Communications

Currency
1 Dalmatia's official currency is the Croatian kuna (kn or HRK). There are 100 lipa to the kuna, though the former are effectively obsolete. Prices are often quoted in euros and kuna, with both accepted. Exchange rates are often more favourable for kuna than euros.

Exchange
2 Banks, post offices, *bureaux de change*, travel agencies and hotels all offer exchange services, with the euro being the most easily converted currency. Many will also readily exchange US dollars and sterling for kuna. Most banks and post offices also change travellers' cheques. Banks offer the best deal for currency exchange.

Cash Machines
3 Cities, towns and larger villages have ATMs. You can use credit and debit cards to withdraw money at an ATM, and will pay commission or a set fee each time you do so. ATMs are few and far between in rural locations and on smaller islands.

Credit Cards and Debit Cards
4 American Express, Diners Club, MasterCard, Visa, Maestro and Cirrus are widely accepted in shops, restaurants and hotels, as well as at ATMs, although it's wise to keep some spare cash on you *(see*

p106). Before travelling, check with your issuer for hidden charges and note the international number for reporting a lost or stolen card. Chip-and-pin technology is increasingly common.

Public Phones
5 Direct calls can be made to local, national and international numbers using any public phone. Most only work with a phone card, which can be bought at a post office or from a tobacco kiosk in denominations of 25 to 500 units. For local calls, omit the three-digit area code. The country code for Croatia is 385.

Mobile Phones
6 Mobile phone calls made within Croatia are charged at local mobile rates, but the cost of incoming and outgoing international calls is high. Phone calls made from Croatian numbers to mobiles on global networks also incur expensive international charges. Those visiting for a long time should consider purchasing a Croatian SIM card.

Post Offices
7 At larger post offices you can post mail, send faxes, buy telephone cards, exchange currency, withdraw cash using a credit card and arrange Western Union money transfers. Airmail takes around five days to reach

Europe and two weeks to reach the USA. Normal opening hours are 7am to 7pm Monday to Friday, 7am to 1pm on Saturday. Branches in small towns often close earlier.

Internet
8 Internet cafés have sprung up all over Dalmatia. Coin-operated terminals are common in hotel lobbies. Wireless technology is arriving, with hotspots appearing in a growing number of hotels and cafés; VIP runs the biggest network.
 VIP: www.vipnet.hr

Television
9 State-owned Hrvatska Radio Televizija (HRT) broadcasts on HRT1 and HRT2. Two privately run channels – Nova TV and RTL – have recently gone on air. Non-sub scription satellite channels, mainly in German or Italian, are also widely available. Upmarket hotels will usually have international channels, including BBC World and CNN.

Newspapers
10 Croatian dailies include *Slobodna Dalmacija, Večernji list, Jutarnji list, Vjesnik* and *Hina News Line* (the latter in English). Foreign-language dailies include *The Guardian Europe* and *International Herald Tribune,* but they are often too out-of-date to justify the inflated prices.
 Hina News Line: www. hina.hr

If you are planning to pay by credit card, make sure that you know your chip-and-pin number.

Left **Croatian wines** Right **Duty-free shopping**

Top 10 Eating, Drinking & Shopping Tips

1 Tax refunds
Croatian sales tax, at the rate of 22 per cent, is included in the price of every item. Non-Croatians who spend over 500kn in a single transaction in a shop displaying a "Tax Free Shopping" sign can claim tax back through the Global Refund scheme. Customers need to obtain a Global Refund Cheque at the time of purchase, and ensure that they take this, the original receipt and the goods to the refund desk at the airport.
⬙ www.globalrefund.com

2 Keep Spare Cash
ATMs, banks, post offices and currency exchange bureaus are scarce in rural areas and smaller villages in Dalmatia. Although credit cards and debit cards are becoming more widely accepted, they are not taken everywhere, so keep enough Croatian currency with you to cover accommodation, meals, petrol and other costs for at least a day.

3 Happy Hours
In tourist areas, drinks promotions offering significantly discounted prices are common. Times vary, so check local advertisements.

4 Picnics
Stock up on tasty fare from food markets, supermarkets or directly from local producers (look out for signs), before heading to the beach, waterfront or picnic spot of your choice. Benches are common in beauty spots, but there are few organized picnic facilities. Those planning regular picnics might like to invest in a cooler picnic backpack and a small rug before leaving home.

5 Types of Restaurant
Eateries are traditionally categorized as *restoran* (restaurant), *konoba* (taverna) or *gostiona* (inn). Differences can be hard to define. Broadly speaking, there is a descending degree of formality and a corresponding fall in price from *restoran* down to *gostiona*. In practice, the distinction is blurred. Other places to eat include the *slastičarnica*, which sells cakes and pastries, and ice-cream *(sladoled)* parlours.

6 Opening Hours
As a rule of thumb, shops open from 8am to 9pm Monday to Friday and 8am to 1pm or 2pm on Saturdays. In tourist centres, trading hours are longer, especially in the high season. Smaller shops may take an extended lunch hour.

7 Wine
Some of Croatia's best wine comes from Dalmatia. Look out for dry white wines from Konavle (Maraština and Ragusa), Korčula (Pošip and Rukatac), the Pelješac Peninsula (Sveta Ana), Vis (Vugava) and Hvar (Zlatan Otok and Zavala). Recommended reds come from the Pelješac Peninsula (Dingač, Plavac, Plavac Mali and Postup), Konavle (Merlot and Cabernet Sauvignon) and Hvar (Zlatan Plavac). Northern Dalmatian Babić and Central Dalmatian Kaštelet are other popular red wines. You can cut your costs by buying direct from the vineyard.

8 Cash Discounts
Some shops, hotels and restaurants offer discounts of 10 to 20 per cent if you pay in cash.

9 Duty-free
Croatia is not in the EU, so foreigners can buy a wide range of duty-free items at its airports. Gifts, alcohol, tobacco, perfumes, confectionery, jewellery and leather goods are available. Prices are competitive, but it is often cheaper to buy wine and foodstuffs in local shops.

10 Tipping
Service is normally included in the price of a meal, but it is customary to round the bill up to the nearest 10kn, and to leave an additional tip of 10 to 15 per cent if service has been exceptionally good, especially in tourist areas. Taxi drivers appreciate, but do not expect, a tip.

If you are intending to reclaim the sales tax on items you have purchased in Croatia, don't open them until you have done so.

Left **Multi-lingual accommodation sign** Right **Food market**

🔟 Dalmatia on a Budget

Charter Flights
In season, there are charter flights from all over Europe to Dalmatia. A local travel agent will be able to give details.

Budget Flights
There are currently no budget airlines flying direct to Croatia. Indirect options include flying from London Stansted to Bari or Ancona with Ryanair, then travelling on to Split, Hvar or Dubrovnik by ferry or catamaran *(see p103)*. You can travel overland to Dalmatia from Ljubljana (Slovenia) and Trieste (Italy), but journey times are long (about 16 hours). Check the logistics and cost of transfer before booking budget flights on this basis. WhichBudget has the details of most European budget airline routes. ❧ *www.ryanair.com • www.whichbudget.com*

Packages
The Croatian National Tourist Office can provide a list of travel agents that organize package holidays in Dalmatia. A package can often be cheaper than standard room rates and flight costs, especially if booked at the last minute. ❧ *Croatian National Tourist Office: www.croatia.hr*

Accommodation
To secure the best deals, book well ahead and compare rates on the Internet with quotes taken over the telephone. Share a room if possible, as additional beds can often be added at little extra cost. Touts who solicit for guests at bus and ferry terminals offer cheap private rooms; before agreeing, always check the location. Book private accommodation for three days or more, as a 30 per cent surcharge is often levied for shorter stays. Local travel agents can also arrange affordable rooms or apartments.

Visit out of Season
Most hotels operate three seasonal price-bands: June to September are the peak months, and so the most expensive; in April, May and October, the rates are slightly reduced; in November and March, prices can be significantly cheaper, even in Dubrovnik.

Food
Using self-catering accommodation equipped with a fridge and cooker is one way to save money on food. Many camp sites also have electrical points, where appliances can be plugged in. Produce from local shops and markets is generally cheaper than that in supermarkets. Many restaurants in the region are good value.

Markets
As well as cheap fresh fruit, vegetables, fish and other groceries, markets in tourist areas often sell some souvenirs and foodstuffs such as honey, spirits and olive oil, which make good gifts. Try them also for clothing, leather goods or a tasty snack.

Transport
Long-distance bus fares on boats are both reasonable. For families and larger groups, the convenience of hiring a car *(see p103)* may outweigh the savings to be made after purchasing multiple tickets. On local bus services buy tickets in advance as this is often cheaper than obtaining them from the driver.

Internal Flights
Flying from the capital Zagreb to Split, Dubrovnik, Zadar or (in the peak season only) the island of Brač saves valuable time. Once in Croatia, foreigners can book Croatia Airlines flights at their offices at discounted local rates. ❧ *www.croatiaairlines.hr*

Sightseeing
Dalmatia offers plenty of free activities: visiting churches, exploring the narrow lanes of the old towns, walking and swimming (from most beaches). Galleries exhibiting the work of Croatian and international artists also welcome visitors without charge. There is usually a nominal fee to visit museums, with discounts given for children and family tickets sometimes available.

Left **Photographic restaurant menus** Right **Old-town driving**

🔟 Things to Avoid

1 Cruise Ship Crowds

Dubrovnik and Split can be overrun when a cruise ship (or two) docks and its passengers come ashore, usually in the afternoon. To avoid trailing around attractions after large tour groups, or struggling to get a seat in a restaurant, spend your afternoons relaxing in your hotel, on the beach or exploring sights beyond the city centre. At night, when the cruise ships have left, a much quieter old town awaits.

2 Tourist Restaurants

Beware of restaurants with photographic menus and staff soliciting your custom – both warning signs that local people don't eat there. Expecting your patronage only once, such establishments will often serve up bland and lacklustre food. Dalmatians rarely eat out, except when on business and for special occasions: local accents are the sign of a good restaurant.

3 Adriatic Highway

The main road that runs along the length of the Adriatic coast, the Adriatic Highway (Jadranska Magistrala), can be a nightmare to drive on between June and September. Coaches, freight vehicles, slow-driving tourists and locals in a hurry, combined with a single lane road, are a recipe for traffic jams and accidents. A new motorway linking Zadar, Šibenik and Split to Zagreb, and the widening of the Adriatic Highway itself, are improving the situation, but it remains a dangerous and busy road.

4 Driving in Old Towns

Large sections of the region's old towns are pedestrianized and if you try, like some locals, to drive through them you may get stuck behind parked cars, or find yourself at a dead end that it is hard to reverse out of. It is much easier to use the car parks located just outside the old towns and walk in.

5 Regional Politics

In a region that was badly hit by war during the early 1990s, it is not surprising that many Dalmatians still feel passionately about this subject. Entering into idle conversation about people's experiences of the war can be seen as prying. Debating the rights and wrongs of the conflict won't win you friends either. However, genuine interest in what took place here will often elicit illuminating, even harrowing, stories.

6 Language Faux Pas

To the untrained ear the Croatian language sounds very similar to the Slavic tongues of its neighbours, particularly Slovenian and Serbian. Although they may understand it, Croatians do not appreciate people using Slovene or Serb vocabulary; for instance, be careful not to confuse Croatian *molim* (please) with Slovenian *prosim*.

7 Over-exposure to the Sun

Cooling sea breezes and mountain winds can mask the power of the sun. Serious sunburn will need medical treatment and can ruin your trip, so take sensible precautions at all times *(see p104)*. Where possible, sit in the shade or under a parasol.

8 Visiting Museums on Mondays

Many museums are open seven days a week. Those that do close will usually do so on a Monday.

9 Schoolchildren

In April schoolchildren from all over Croatia seem to converge on the tourist centres, with Dubrovnik being the hot favourite. They are usually well behaved, but they can take up all the space in a museum or church, and are hard to keep out of your photographs.

10 Pickpockets

While crime rates in Dalmatia are low *(see p104)*, petty theft is on the rise. Where possible keep valuables in inside or zipped pockets.

View from the Excelsior, Dubrovnik *(see p110)*

🔟 Accommodation Tips

1 Price and Location
Annoyingly, the closer it is to the Old Town, the more expensive the room. A good compromise is to stay outside the centre where transport links are good (as in Split and Dubrovnik) and splash out on old-town rooms the rest of the time.

2 A Room with a View
Dalmatia is brimming with hotels that overlook the sea. Rooms with a sea view come at a small extra cost, but when the choice is between looking out onto the sea or car park, it is worth finding the extra funds. Specify at the time of booking that you want a sea view, to avoid being disappointed on arrival.

3 Beware of Noise
At the height of the tourist season hotels located next to cafés and bars can suddenly become noisy, when stereos pump out tunes until the small hours. If you are uncertain about the hotel's location ask about possible disturbances before booking.

4 Grading Systems
Croatian hotels are classified from basic 1-star up to luxurious 5-star. In 1- and 2-star hotels, some rooms may have shared bathrooms. This grading system can also broadly be applied to private accommodation.

A renovation programme is gradually bringing all Dalmatian hotels up to 3-star standard or above.

5 Lighthouses
For a break with a difference consider staying in one of seven historic stone lighthouses located on Dalmatia's most remote islands and islets *(see p115)*. Choosing the lighthouse carefully can save on the cost of private transfers, with Veli Rat (Dugi Otok), Struga (Lastovo) and Sv Petar (on the mainland near Makarska) accessible by public transport or car. Renting is usually by the week, but between mid-September and early May you may be able to book two-day stays. Contact Plovput for more details. 🌐 www.plovput.hr

6 Rural Hotels
The agritourism concept of farm holidays is slowly emerging here. Villagers in the likes of Šibenik-Knin county, close to Krka National Park, are opening their doors to tourists. Properties are usually simple and clean, with many retaining rustic elements. Prices are roughly equivalent to that of a private room in a coastal town or city.

7 Children
Self-contained apartments arranged through local and national travel agencies can be good value for families *(see*

p116–17). Most hotels will provide a baby's cot for a small daily charge.

8 Peak Season
Hotels, apartments, rooms and camp sites are in high demand, and at their most expensive from June to September *(see p107)*; some places hike up their prices even further in July and August. It is easier, and cheaper, to secure accommodation without a reservation in April and October. From November to March rates are at their lowest, but many hotels, and most camp sites, are closed.

9 Internet Booking
The Internet can be a useful tool when choosing accommodation, allowing you to view photographs, read reviews submitted by previous guests and compare prices, before making a booking. Some hotels and one-stop booking sites discount rates, particularly when there is late availability.

10 Breakfast, Half-board and Full-board
Most hotel rates include breakfast. Even upmarket hotels often offer half-board, but full-board is rarer. Dalmatia has an abundance of fine and inexpensive eateries, so unless budget is your prime concern think twice about committing to dining in the hotel.

Left **Swimming pool at the Argentina** Right **Bedroom at the Dubrovnik President**

TOP10 Dubrovnik Hotels

Excelsior
Easily the finest hotel in Dubrovnik in the years since the war of the 90s, the Excelsior keeps ahead of its rivals by constantly upgrading its facilities. The setting is superb too, with stunning Old City views from many of the rooms. ✆ Frana Supila 12 • Map M5 • 020 353 353 • www.hotel-excelsior.hr • KKKKK

Dubrovnik Palace
A renovation in 2004 brought luxury and a first-rate spa to this large hotel on the Lapad Peninsula. All bedrooms have balconies and sea views. Leisure facilities include indoor and outdoor pools. ✆ Masarykov Put 20 • Map K4 • 020 430 000 • www.dubrovnikpalace.hr • KKKKK

Argentina
Recently restored to its full 5-star glory, the Argentina is in the district of Ploče (just east of the gate of the same name). Choose a room in the main hotel or in one of four villas. The sea-view rooms enjoy fabulous views of the Old City. ✆ Frana Supila 14 • Map M5 • 020 440 555 • www.gva.hr • KKKKK

Hilton Imperial
The former Imperial Hotel, just outside the Pile Gate, reopened its doors after a long wait in 2005, as the Hilton Imperial. A fitness centre, indoor pool and all the services that you would expect from this chain are complemented by a warm Mediterranean decor and views of the Old City. ✆ Marijana Blazića 2 • Map G5 • 020 320 320 • www.hilton.com • KKKKK

Dubrovnik
A small hotel, with just 28 clean and simply furnished rooms (4 of them suites), Dubrovnik is a welcome change from the larger hotels that dominate the Lapad Peninsula. It has a nice café-bar. ✆ Šetalište Kralja Zvonimira bb • Map L4 • 020 435 030 • www.hoteldubrovnik.hr • KK

Bellevue
Just 15 minutes' walk from the Old City, this appealing 2-star hotel overlooks the attractive Miramare Bay. Sea-view rooms with balconies are worth the extra €11. It has a private beach and is soon to have a refurbishment that will transform it into a luxurious 5-star hotel. ✆ Pera Čingrije 7 • Map L4 • 020 413 306 • www.hotel-bellevue.hr • No air con • KK

Uvala
This stylish Lapad hotel has indoor and outdoor pools, a "wellness" centre, private parking and conference facilities. The 51 rooms are minimalist, with white walls and beige soft furnishings. Some are sea-facing; all offer creature comforts like slippers and bath robes. ✆ Masarykov Put 6 • Map L4 • 020 433 580 • www.hotelimaestral.com • KKKKK

Kompas
Slated for a major refit designed to bring it up to 4-star standard, for now Kompas is a cheaper option located above Uvala Bay beach and with views of the sea. The balconied rooms will offer greater comfort in the future. ✆ Šetalište Kralja Zvonimira 56 • Map L4 • 020 352 000 • www.hotel-kompas.hr • KKK

Dubrovnik President
This large, concrete hotel is redeemed by the fact that all its well-equipped balconied rooms are sea-facing and offer views of the Elafiti Islands. A private beach, indoor pool, sports facilities and its proximity to Copacabana Beach (see p66) are also plus points. ✆ Iva Dulčića 39 • Map K4 • 020 441 100 • www.babinkuk.com • KKKK

Lero
The good-value Lero is located 15 minutes' walk from the Old City. Close to the beach, it has clean, simply decorated rooms (many with sea views) with white walls and bedding. The guest parking is a useful bonus. ✆ Put Iva Vojnovića 14 • Map L4 • 020 341 333 • www.hotel-lero.hr • KK

For the Lapad Peninsula **See p66**; for more hotels in Dubrovnik **See p114**

Jadran, Šibenik

Price Categories

For a standard double room per night (with breakfast if included), taxes and extra charges.

K	under 450kn
KK	450–900kn
KKK	900–1,350kn
KKKK	1,350–1,800kn
KKKKK	over 1,800kn

🔟 Northern Dalmatian Hotels

1 Biser, Pag
The small, family-run Biser is 2 km (1 mile) from the centre of Pag Town. Some of its 24 rooms have stunning views over Pag Bay and the Velebit Mountains. With a car park, an on-site restaurant, tennis courts and a private beach in a pleasant cove, the Biser is ideal for families. 🕾 *Antuna Gustava Matoša 46 • Map A2 • 023 611 333 • www. hotel-biser.com • KK*

2 Pagus, Pag
This low-rise resort-style hotel has a superb location just northwest of Pag Town. Simple rooms have balconies, with the best boasting sea views. 🕾 *Ante Starčevića 1 • Map A2 • 023 611 310 • www. coning.hr • Closed mid-Oct–Apr • KK*

3 Alan, Starigrad-Paklenica
Housed in an unappealing tower block, the Alan is a blot on the landscape, but its rooms (which sleep up to six) were upgraded to 3-star standard in 2003. A camp site, restaurant, café, outdoor pool, and its proximity to the beach attract families. 🕾 *Dr Fanje Tuđmana 14 • Map B2 • 023 209 050 • www. bluesunhotels.com • Closed Nov–mid-Mar • KK*

4 Vicko, Starigrad-Paklenica
This welcoming family-run hotel has recently added 4-star seaside rooms to its existing 3-star accommodation. An attractive terrace restaurant serving good food adds to the hotel's charm. Splash out on one of the new Villa Vicko suites, with balconies overlooking the sea and the Paklenica mountains. 🕾 *Jože Dokoze 20 • Map B2 • 023 369 304 • www. hotel-vicko.hr • KKK*

5 Kolovare, Zadar
This business-oriented hotel has an outdoor pool and modern rooms, and is close to the beach. Just 10 minutes' walk from Zadar's old town, its location is hard to beat, but prices are on the high side for a 3-star hotel. 🕾 *Bože Peričića 14 • Map B3 • 023 203 200 • www.hotel-kolovare-zadar. htnet.hr • KKK*

6 Skradinski Buk, Skradin
This attractive hotel has 28 simple, comfortable rooms in which yellow bedding and prints add a splash of colour. In-room facilities include mini-bars, satellite TV and Internet points. All rooms have balconies. 🕾 *Skradin • Map C4 • 022 771 771 • www. skradinskibuk.hr • KK*

7 Movie Resort Hotel, Tribunj
Guests staying in the 28 well-equipped rooms, named after film stars, have access to a private beach and the British-style Movie Pub, which serves food. There is also an apartment annex. 🕾 *Jurjevgradska 49 • Map C4 • 022 446 331 • www. themovieresort.com • Closed Jan–Apr • KKK*

8 Jadran, Šibenik
Šibenik's only centrally located hotel has recently been given a make over to provide guests with light, modern and comfortable rooms. A pleasant pavement café, mini-bars, private car parking and sea-facing rooms also stand in its favour. 🕾 *Doktora Franje Tuđmana 52 • Map C4 • 022 242 000 • www. rivijera.hr • KK*

9 Panorama, Šibenik
As its name suggests, one of the main reasons to stay here is for the view, with some south-facing rooms overlooking the Šibenik archipelago and the city's old town. Recently refurbished. 🕾 *Šibenski Most bb • Map C4 • 022 213 397 • www. hotel-panorama.hr • KK*

10 Villa Koša, Primošten
The 13 individually styled units at this aparthotel vary in size, sleeping between two and eight. Most have balconies and sea views; some have small kitchenettes. Breakfast and air conditioning are charged on top of the room rate. 🕾 *Josip Bana Jelačića 4 • Map C4 • 022 570 365 • www.villa-kosa. htnet.hr • KK*

> **Note:** Unless otherwise stated, all hotels accept credit cards and have ensuite bathrooms and air conditioning.

Left **Slavija, Split** Right **Paula, Vis Town**

ⁱ⁰ Central Dalmatian Hotels

Slavija, Split

A serious injection of cash has transformed a formerly grungy dive into this clean and welcoming 3-star hotel. Set inside Diocletian's palace, it has simply furnished en-suite rooms. If you can afford it, splash out on suite 401, with its separate sitting area. ⓈBuvinina 2 • Map P2 • 021 323 840 • www. hotelslavija.com • KK

Park, Split

Traditionally regarded as Split's best hotel, the Park is just set back from the waterfront at Bačvice. It boasts comfortable modern rooms, friendly staff and a decent restaurant with a palm-fringed terrace looking out to sea. ⓈHatzov Perivoj 3 • Map Q6 • 021 406 400 • www. hotelpark-split.hr • KKK

Split, Split

Located 40 minutes' walk from the old town, the position of the Split deters some guests, though the stroll around the bay is pleasant and its rooms are light and spacious. Book a room with a balcony and sea view. The hotel has its own beach, outdoor pool and parking. ⓈPut Trstenika 19 • off map • 021 303 111 • www. hotelsplit.hr • KKK

Bellevue, Split

The simple rooms at the Bellevue are light and of a good size. Some have views out towards Split's waterfront, others onto the attractive Austro-Hungarian influenced square. The café spills out onto Trg Republike and is a pleasant place to while away an hour or so. ⓈBana Jelačića 2 • Map N2 • 021 345 644 • www. hotel-bellevue-split.hr • No air con • KK

Fontana, Trogir

This old-town hotel offers large, if slightly old-fashioned, rooms. Those with a Jacuzzi are worth the extra charge and the hotel's well-equipped apartment suits families. ⓈObrov 1 • Map D5 • 021 885 744 • www.fontana-commerce.htnet.hr • KK

Vila Sikaa, Čiovo

There are 10 bright, up-to-date rooms and suites at this family-run boutique hotel. Some offer stunning views of Trogir's old town, while others have wooden beams. All rooms have mini-bars and Internet connections and the executive double has a Jacuzzi. ⓈObala Kralja Zvonimira 13 • Map D5 • 021 881 223 • www. vila-sikaa-r.com • KK

Paula, Vis Town

The historic Kut area of Vis Town is the setting for this small, family-owned hotel. Its stone façade, large guest rooms, tranquil location and excellent seafood restaurant are a winning combination. Some rooms have views to the sea. ⓈPetra Hektrovica 2 • Map D6 • 021 711 362 • www. paula-hotel.t-com.hr • KKK

Amfora, Hvar Town

Hvar's largest hotel is staggering in its scale. Welcoming staff, pleasant bedrooms, many with views of the Pakleni Islands (see p84), and diverse sports facilities, including a large indoor pool, are among its plus points. It is one of the few hotels in Hvar Town open year round. ⓈDolac bb • Map D6 • 021 750 300 • www.suncanihvar.hr • KK

Palace, Hvar Town

This well-equipped 3-star hotel is housed in a Venetian-style villa in the centre of Hvar Town. From the terrace with its stone-carved balustrade you can watch the bustle of daily life, and yachts anchoring in the harbour. ⓈTrg Sv Stjepana bb • Map D6 • 021 741 966 • www.suncani hvar. hr • No air con • KK

Riva, Hvar Town

In an attractive stone building overlooking Hvar Town's marina, the 4-star Riva has simple, comfortable accommodation with air conditioning, and is open year-round. Try to bag a sea-facing room with a balcony. A word of warning: adjacent to a lively bar, the hotel is not for light sleepers. ⓈRiva • Map D6 • 021 750 100 • www.suncanihvar.hr • KKKK

Note: Unless otherwise stated, all hotels accept credit cards and have en-suite bathrooms and air conditioning.

Price Categories		
For a standard double room per night (with breakfast if included), taxes and extra charges.	**K**	under 450kn
	KK	450–900kn
	KKK	900–1,350kn
	KKKK	1,350–1,800kn
	KKKKK	over 1,800kn

Liburna, Korčula Town

🔟 Southern Dalmatian Hotels

Liburna, Korčula Town
Winning features of this pleasant 3-star hotel include its outdoor pool, tennis courts, mini-golf, water sports, bicycle hire and car park. The ten per cent surcharge for a room with views of the old town, pool and terrace is well worth it. ⊗ *Put od Luke 17 • Map H1 • 020 726 006 • www. korcula-hotels.com • No air con • KKK*

Korčula, Korčula Town
Korčula Town's most central hotel occupies an old building with a charming terrace over-looking the west harbour. Rooms are reasonable, not outstanding. ⊗ *Obala Dr Franje Tudmana 5 • Map H1 • 020 711 078 • www. korcula-hotels.com • No air con • KKK*

Ostrea, Mali Ston
Framed by the sea and the Pelješac hills, the Ostrea is an attractive small hotel in the former home of its proprietors, the Kralj family. Modern art adorns plain walls in the tasteful rooms and suite. ⊗ *Ante Starčevića 9 • Map K2 • 020 754 555 • www.ostrea.hr • KK*

Vila Koruna, Mali Ston
This family-run restaurant with rooms is set on the shore of the Malo Stonski Channel. Stressed city-dwellers and amorous

couples flock here from all over Croatia to enjoy the fine seafood, stunning scenery and tranquillity. ⊗ *Pelješki Put • Map K2 • 020 754 999 • www. vila-koruna.hr • KK*

Bellevue, Orebić
An unmistakable red façade adorns this relaxed 2-star resort hotel. Just northwest of the town centre, it is shaded by pines and close to a pebble beach. There is an annexe and apartment block. Most rooms have sea views; try to book one with a balcony. ⊗ *Sveti Križa 104 • Map H1 • 020 713 148 • www.orebic-htp. hr • No air con • K*

Castel Antonia, Orebić
This welcoming villa, built in a slightly kitsch castle style, luxuriates amid lush vegetation on the Pelješac Peninsula, with dramatic land and sea views from its terraces and balconies. There are 19 rooms and apartments, bar and restaurant. ⊗ *Poštup, Pelješac Peninsula • Map H1 • 020 713 464 • www.villa-antonio.de • KK*

Croatia, Cavtat
Everything you would expect to find at a colossal 5-star resort hotel is available at the Croatia: a fitness centre, sports facilities galore, a private beach, and indoor, outdoor and children's pools. All rooms are large and have balconies (many

with sea views) and baths. ⊗ *Frankopanska 10 • Map L3 • 020 475 555 • www. hoteli-croatia.hr • KKKK*

Villa Kvaternik, Cavtat
This luxurious boutique hotel is housed in a 15th-century stone building at the heart of Cavtat's old town. It has 6 rooms with wooden floors and bright, modern soft furnishings. In-room facilities include Internet connections. Try to get a room with a view of the bay. ⊗ *Kvaternikova 3 • Map L3 • 020 479 800 • www.dub-iz.hr • KKK*

Monastery, Cavtat
The Australian owners of the Villa Kvaternik also have rooms in the town's former monastery, located right on the waterfront. Single, twin, double and triple rooms are available. Breakfast is served at the Kvaternik, and guests may use the hotel's facililties. ⊗ *Kvaternikova 3 • Map L3 • 020 479 800 • www. dub-iz.hr • No air con • KK*

Villa Neretva, Metković
Right at the heart of the Neretva Delta *(see p90)*, this waterfront restaurant with rooms provides clean and comfortable accom-modation, and has a well-regarded kitchen. It is a good base for exploring this extraordinary water-scape, and runs boat tours for guests. ⊗ *Map J1 • 020 672 200 • www.restaurant-villa-neretva.hr • K*

For more places to stay in Central and Southern Dalmatia
See pp114–15

Left **Peristil, Split** Right **Villa Dubrovnik, Dubrovnik**

🔟 Characterful Hotels

1 Pučić Palace, Dubrovnik

Classical elegance and history pervade every aspect of this refurbished Renaissance palace. Be the envy of everyone in Dubrovnik by staying in the only luxury hotel within the Old City walls. ✆ Od Puča 1 • Map J5 • 020 326 200 • www.the pucicpalace.com • KKKKK

2 Villa Orsula, Dubrovnik

This palatial waterfront villa is the choice of the discerning traveller. In a separate building, the villa is more intimate than the rest of the Argentina Hotel *(see p110)* and a cut above most Dubrovnik accommodation. Some rooms have balconies overlooking the Old City and all have an elegant classical decor. ✆ Frana Supila 14 • Map M5 • 020 440 555 • www.gva.hr • KKKKK

3 Villa Wolff, Dubrovnik

This 6-room boutique hotel offers pleasant rooms, attentive service and a restaurant with sea views, as well as a wonderfully lush garden. ✆ Nika I Meda Pučića 1 • Map L4 • 020 435 353 • www.villa-wolff.hr • KKKK

4 Villa Dubrovnik, Dubrovnik

Situated in a green oasis removed from the hustle and bustle of the Old City is this tranquil and luxurious retreat. Its comfortable rooms have balconies with views of the sea and Dubrovnik. The boat shuttle service into the Old Harbour adds that extra element of romance. ✆ Vlaha Bukovca 6 • Map M5 • 020 422 933 • www. villa-dubrovnik.hr • KKKKK

5 Stari Grad Hotel, Dubrovnik

The cheaper of the two hotels in the Old City, this intimate, 8-roomed establishment is tucked away in a narrow street just off the Stradun. The highlight here is the roof terrace, which provides prime views of the historic centre and is a great spot for people-watching. ✆ Od Sigurate 4 • Map H5 • 020 322 244 • www. hotelstarigrad.com • KKKK

6 President, Zadar

Elegance and good service are the order of the day at this boutique hotel located northwest of Zadar's old town in Borik. Dark woods and hues of beige and brown lend a classical feel to the well-equipped rooms. A 45-minute coastal walk leads to the old town. ✆ Desnice 16 • Map B3 • 023 333 696 • www. hotel-president.hr • KKKK

7 Ivan, Bol, Brač

This traditional stone building in the heart of Bol has been reinvented as a chic, family-run hotel. The spa, outdoor pool and rooms with views across to the island of Hvar all add to its charm. ✆ David 11a • Map E5 • 021 640 888 • www. hotel-ivan.com • KKK

8 Palača Dešković, Pučišća, Brač

Tucked away on Brač's northern shore is one of the region's most upscale establishments. Housed in a former 15th-century palace, this intimate hotel has moorings for yachts, a restaurant serving traditional meals and an attractive courtyard and garden. ✆ Map E5 • 021 778 240 • www. palaca-deskovic.com • KKK

9 Peristil, Split

The latest addition to Split's hotel scene,the Peristil has 12 individually styled rooms at the heart of Diocletian's Palace. The decor is light and elegant throughout, while friendly staff provide the finishing touch. Book room 304, or one overlooking the Peristyle *(see p22)*. ✆ Poljana Kraljice Jelene 5 • Map Q2 • 021 329 070 • www. hotelperistil.com • KK

10 Adriana, Split

Its prime waterfront location on the Riva *(see p24)* and its clean, modern rooms have made this small hotel one of Split's most popular – so book well in advance. ✆ Obla Hrvatskog Narodnog Preporoda 8 (Riva) • Map N2 • 021 340 000 • www. hotel-adriana.hr • KK

Note: Unless otherwise stated, all hotels accept credit cards and have en-suite bathrooms and air conditioning.

Stone Cottages, Kornati Islands

Price Categories

For a standard	**K**	under 450kn
double room per	**KK**	450–900kn
night (with breakfast	**KKK**	900–1,350kn
if included), taxes	**KKKK**	1,350–1,800kn
and extra charges.	**KKKKK**	over 1,800kn

🔟 Island Retreats

1 Palagruža Lighthouse

To really get away from it all, head to Croatia's most remote lighthouse, located on an island 68 nautical miles from Split. At 90 m (295 ft) above sea level, it offers superb views over the Adriatic and the little island itself. Transfer from Korčula Town costs about 350kn. ✆ off map • www.light houses-penul.com • KKK

2 Pločica Lighthouse

Built in 1887, this automated lighthouse can accommodate 14 people in two apartments. The flat islet, between Hvar, Korčula and the Pelješac Peninsula, is ideal for swimming and diving. Transfer from Korčula Town costs about 900kn. ✆ Map G1 • www.light houses-penul.com • KKK

3 Prišnjak Lighthouse, Murter

Situated on an islet just off Murter, the Prišnjak lighthouse can be easily reached by yacht. While it doesn't offer a sense of remoteness, transfers are reasonably priced (around 370kn), and supplies can be delivered daily. ✆ Map B4 • www.light houses-penul.com • KKK

4 Struga Lighthouse, Lastovo

The four apartments in this attractive 1839 lighthouse can sleep two to five people. Situated 5 km (3 miles) from Lastovo Town, it can be reached by road, but residents are hardly likely to be disturbed by tourist hordes on this remote island. ✆ Struga Cape • Map G2 • www.light houses-penul.com • KKK

5 Sušac Lighthouse

Contructed from Dalmatian stone in 1878, this lighthouse has two apartments, each of which sleeps four people. At an elevation of 100 m (328 ft) above sea level, it is a good vantage point. Tranquillity is assured on this uninhabited island. ✆ Map G2 • www.light houses-penul.com • KKK

6 Veli Rat Lighthouse, Dugi Otok

Perfect for those who want peace and quiet but also want access to local facilities, Veli Rat light house is situated 3 km (2 miles) from two villages on the island of Dugi Otok and accessible by road. ✆ Map A3 • www.light houses-penul.com • KKK

7 Stone Cottages, Kornati Islands

A number of tourist agencies in Murter have a portfolio of rustic stone houses in the Kornati Islands National Park, where you can live out a desert island dream. Even if the island is not totally deserted, it can certainly feel like it is. You can arrange to have supplies dropped off every few days. ✆ Map B4 • Coronata: www. coronata.hr; Kornat Turist: www.kornatturist.hr; Žut Tours: www.zuttours.hr • No credit cards • KK

8 Hotel Odisej, Mljet National Park

This large, whitewashed resort hotel is set in the heart of Mljet National Park. Rooms are fairly basic; the apartment is more luxurious. The hotel has a beach, tavern and marina, but the real draw is the stunning setting. ✆ Pomena • Map J2 • 020 744 022 • www. hotelodisej.com • KK

9 Hotel Šipan, Šipan

This 80-room hotel overlooks a tranquil bay on the largest of the Elafiti Islands. It has two restaurants and a bar. Close to beaches and secluded coves, it offers a great escape from the mid-summer hustle and bustle of Dubrovnik. ✆ Map K2 • 020 758 000 • www.sipanhotel.com • No air con • Closed mid-Oct– Apr • KK

10 Hotel Villa Vilina, Lopud

This 4-star hotel occupies a villa shrouded by lush vegetation beside the marina. It has 14 rooms and three suites, all modern and elegant. The restaurant, with its sea-view terrace, is popular. ✆ Obala Ivana Kuljevana 5 Map K2 • 020 759 333 • www.villa-vilina.hr • KKK

Note: The lighthouses have no en-suite bathrooms or air con; their pricing is derived from the weekly rate per unit divided by seven.

115

Left **Dubrovnik Youth Hostel** Right **Karmen Apartments, Dubrovnik**

🔟 Budget Accommodation

1 Dubrovnik Youth Hostel
A 10-minute walk from the main bus station and 15 minutes from the Old City, Dubrovnik's 82-bed hostel is clean and welcoming. Accommodation is in bunks within male and female dormitories. Reservations are a must. ◈ *Vinka Sagrestana 3 • Map L4 • 020 423 241 • www.hfhs.hr • No en-suite • No air con • K*

2 Adriatic, Dubrovnik
One of Dubrovnik's few remaining 2-star hotels, and one of the city's more affordable options, the Adriatic is still by no means cheap. The hotel has a fairly rudimentary gym and clay tennis courts; it is also well located for the beach. ◈ *Masarykov Put 9 • Map L4 • 020 433 520 • www. hotelimaestral.com • KK*

3 Lapad, Dubrovnik
The best thing about this large Lapad Peninsula hotel is the price – but note that you will pay a premium for a room with balcony, sea views and air conditioning. There's an outdoor pool, but it's located quite close to the road. ◈ *Lapadska Obala 37 • Map L4 • 020 432 922 • www.hotel-lapad.hr • No air con • Closed Nov–Apr • KK*

4 Vila Micika, Dubrovnik
Simple accommodation is on offer here in a typically Dalmatian stone villa in Lapad. There are just seven bedrooms, so book well in advance. The villa has a car park and a communal terrace. ◈ *Mate Vodopica 10 • Map L4 • 020 437 332 • www. vilamicika.hr • No air con • K*

5 Karmen Apartments, Dubrovnik
These individually styled, well-equipped apartments enjoy a prime location inside the Old City walls. Book room 1, overlooking the old port, and be the envy of every tourist who passes. Considering their position, the apartments represent good value. ◈ *Bandureva 1 • Map K6 • 020 323 433 • www. karmendu.tk • KK*

6 Zagreb, Dubrovnik
The 3-star Zagreb stands out from the mass of hotels in Lapad due to its size (it has just 23 rooms) and the fact that it is housed not in a concrete block but in an attractive period property. Just 5 minutes from the beach, this is a good budget option. ◈ *Šetalište Kralja Zvonimira 27 • Map L4 • 020 438 930 • www. hotels-sumratin.com   KK*

7 Zadar Youth Hostel
Zadar's modern 290-bed hostel is in the suburb of Borik, 5 km (3 miles) from the historic centre. It has its own sports ground, restaurant and bar. Reservations are recommended in high season. ◈ *Obala Kneza Trpimira 76 • Map B3 • 023 331 145 • www.hfhs.hr • No en-suite • No air con • K*

8 Perin Dvor, Nin
Located by the Donji Most (Lower Bridge), this friendly Croatian-German place has seven rooms and three apartments. The latter have small, fully equipped kitchens, and separate sitting/dining areas. Breakfast (served in the restaurant) costs extra. ◈ *Hrvatskog Sabora 1 • Map B3 • 023 264 307 • K*

9 Accommodation Touts
Locals tout for business at bus and ferry terminals throughout Dalmatia. A private double room will typically cost only 200kn, and can be a good option. Remember to ask to see photographs and the location on a map before accepting, as quality and accessibility vary greatly.

10 Local Tourist Agencies
Many individuals offer private accommodation through tourist agencies. If you call at doors showing *sobe* (rooms) signs, it is common to be directed to these centrally located offices. Staff can be reluctant to help if you plan to stay in the accommodation for less than three days, but persistence can pay off.

Price Categories

For accommodation for two people per night (with breakfast if included), taxes and extra charges.

K	under 450kn
KK	450–900kn
KKK	900–1,350kn
KKKK	1,350–1,800kn
KKKKK	over 1,800kn

Camping Trsteno, Trsteno

🔟 Self-catering & Campsites

1 Camping Solitudo, Dubrovnik

The closest campsite to Dubrovnik's Old City is just a 10-minute bus ride away. It has 238 pitches, a modest restaurant and an outdoor swimming pool. Surrounded by pine trees, it is 200 m (650 ft) from the shore. There are reduced rates for under 12s, making this a popular family option. ✆ *Vatroslava Lisinskog 17* • *Map L4* • *020 448 686* • *www.babinkuk.com* • *Closed mid-Oct–Mar* • K

2 Camping Kalac, Korčula Town

Just 2 km (1 mile) from the historic centre of Korčula Town and 50 m (160 ft) from a beach, this campsite accommodates up to 600 people. Its facilities include a shop and a restaurant. Under 12s pay a reduced rate. There is a small extra charge for parking. ✆ *Adjacent to Bon Repos Hotel* • *Map H1* • *020 711 182* • *www.korcula.net* • *Closed Oct–May* • K

3 Camping Trsteno, Trsteno

Located up the hill from the Trsteno Arboretum, this pleasant small-scale campsite is situated amid olive groves. Stairs provide access for guests to a pebble beach. On-site facilities include a shop and a restaurant. ✆ *Potok 4* • *Map K2* • *020 751 060* • *Closed Oct–Mar* • K

4 Camping Solaris, Šibenik

This campsite's 500-plus spaces are part of the sprawling Solaris Holiday Resort. Camping Solaris itself enjoys a pleasant location amid pine trees just 50 m (160 ft) from the sea. The campsite may never feel exclusive, but guests can use the resort's myriad facilities, including its indoor and outdoor pools. ✆ *Hot Naselje Solaris bb* • *Map C4* • *022 364 000* • *www.solaris.hr* • *Closed Nov–mid-Mar* • K

5 Camping Adriatic, Orebić

A blissfully small campsite by Dalmatian standards, the Adriatic has spaces for just 60 tents or motor homes. Nestling among pine and olive trees, it is set back from a pebble beach and has good views across to Korčula. ✆ *Mokola 6* • *Map H1* • *020 713 420* • *www.adriatic-mikulic.hr* • *Closed Oct–Mar* • K

6 Croatian Villas

This London-based agent arranges rentals throughout Croatia. The company's portfolio of properties on Dalmatia's mainland and islands is extensive. Villas and apartments vary in size, typically accommodating between two and six guests, though larger groups can be catered for. ✆ *020 8888 6655 (UK)* • *www.croatianvillas.com*

7 Tapestry Holidays

You can rent private accommodation on the Pelješac Peninsula, Korčula or Lopud, or in Dubrovnik or Cavtat, through this British company. Properties are selected for their charm, setting and views. ✆ *020 8235 7777 (UK)* • *www.tapestryholidays.com*

8 Dalma Holidays

This Croatian villa rental specialist has just over a dozen, largely seafront properties close to Zadar in the villages of Kožino and Petrčane. All have been finished to a high standard. ✆ *020 8677 2655 (UK)* • *www.dalmaholidays.co.uk*

9 Simply Travel

The emphasis at Simply Travel is on organizing self-catering apartment rentals on the islands of Brač, Hvar, Korčula and Lopud, as well as in Dubrovnik. ✆ *0870 166 4979 (UK)* • *www.simplytravel.co.uk*

10 Croatian Affair

This UK-based company manages a range of attractive private villas and apartments in central and southern Dalmatia. Many of the properties have pools, and most are located in spectacular natural settings. Check out Vrnik Castle on the island of the same name. ✆ *020 7385 7111 (UK)* • *www.croatianaffair.com*

General Index

Index

121

Acknowledgments

The Authors

Based in Scotland, Robin and Jenny McKelvie are a formidable husband-and-wife travel-writing team. Between them they have visited more than 70 countries, and have co-authored guides to Croatia, Latvia, Slovenia and Dubai.

Thanks to the Croatian National Tourist Board, especially Andrea Petrov and Renata Dezeljin in Zagreb, and Josip Lozić in London. Thanks also to Zrinka Marinović and Nikolina Vicelić at Adriatic Luxury Hotels in Dubrovnik.

Produced by DP Services, a division of Duncan Petersen Publishing Ltd.

Editorial Director Chris Barstow
Designer Ian Midson
Copy Editor Jane Oliver-Jedrzejak
Fact-checker Katarina Bulić
Proofreader Antony Mason
Indexer Hilary Bird
Picture Researcher Helen Stallion

Main Photographer Antony Souter
Additional Photography Lucio Rossi, Leandro Zoppé
Illustrator Chapel Design & Marketing
Maps Mapping Ideas Ltd

FOR DORLING KINDERSLEY
Publisher Douglas Amrine
Publishing Managers Kate Poole, Anna Streiffert
Senior Designer Maite Lantaron
Senior Cartographic Editor Casper Morris
Senior DTP Designer Jason Little
Production Controller Linda Dare

Picture Credits

Placement Key: t–top; tc–top centre; tl–top left; tr–top right; cla–centre left above; ca–centre above; cra–centre right above; cl–centre left; c–centre; cr–centre right; clb–centre left below; cb–centre below; crb–centre right below; bl–below left; bc–below centre; br–below right; b–bottom.

Every effort has been made to trace the copyright holders and we apologize in advance for any unintentional omissions. We would be pleased to insert the appropriate acknowledgments in any subsequent edition of this publication.

The publishers would like to thank the following individuals, companies and picture libraries for permission to reproduce their photographs:

ANCIENT ART AND ARCHITECTURE COLLECTION: 25c, 35tr.
ALAMY Jon Arnold 42tr, 70–71; f1 92b, Chris Howes/Wild Places Photography 44tl, Loetscher Chlaus 46tr, Robert Mullan 14–15, Eitan Simanor 52c, Duncan Soar 46c, Swerve 55tl.
BRIDGEMAN: Church of San Marco, Florence, Italy, Giraudon/Bridgeman 25b, Crown Estate 35tl, Palazzo Ducale, Venice, Italy, Cameraphoto Arte Venezia 34tr.
CORBIS: Bettmann 35br, Matko Biljak/Reuters 54tl, Jonathan Blair 54tr, Charles Jean Marc/Sygma 54c, Tim Page 34b.
ROBERT HARDING PICTURE LIBRARY: Travel Library 46tl, 56–57.
REX FEATURES: Sipa Press 34tl.

All other images © Dorling Kindersley. For more information see www.dkimages.com

Phrase Book

Pronounciation Guide

c – "ts" as in rats
ć – "t" as in tube
g – "g" as in get
š – "sh" as in shoe
"aj" – "igh" as in night

č – "ch" as in church
d – "d" as in endure
j – "y" as in yes
ž – "J" as in Jacques

In an Emergency

Help!	**Pomoć!**	**po**moch
Stop!	**Stani!**	**stah**nee
Call a doctor!	**Zovite doktora!**	**zo**veetey **do**ktorah
Call an ambulance!	**Zovite hitnu pomoć!**	**zo**veetey **heet**noo pomoch
Call the police!	**Zovite policiju!**	**zo**veetey poleet**see**yoo
Call the fire brigade!	**Zovite vatrogasce!**	**zo**veetey vatroh**gast**say

Communication Essentials

Yes	**da**	dah
No	**ne**	ney
Please	**molim vas**	**mo**leem vas
Thank you	**hvala**	**hvah**lah
Excuse me	**oprostite**	opros**tee**tey
Hello	**dobar dan**	**do**bar dan
Goodbye	**doviĐenja**	dovee**djen**ya
Good night	**laku noc**	**la**koo noch
Yesterday	**jučer**	**yoo**cher
Today	**danas**	**da**nas
Tomorrow	**sutra**	**soo**trah
Here	**tu**	too
There	**tamo**	**tah**moh
What?	**što?**	shtoh
When?	**kada?**	**ka**da
Why?	**zašto?**	**zash**toh
Where?	**gdje?**	gdyey

Useful Phrases

How are you?	**Kako ste?**	**ka**koh stey
Very well, thank you	**Dobro, hvala**	**do**broh, **hvah**lah
Where is/are...?	**Gdje je/ su?**	gdyey yey/ soo
How can I get to...?	**Kako mogu doći do...?**	kakoh mogoo dochee doh...
Do you speak English?	**Govorite li engleski?**	go**vo**reetey lee **eng**leskee
I don't understand	**Ne razumijem**	nay razoo**mee**eeyem
Could you speak slowly please?	**Molim vas, možete li govoriti sporije?**	**mo**leem vas, **mozh**etey lee go**vo**reetey **spor**yey
I'm sorry	**Žao mi je**	**zha**oh mee yey

Useful Words

big	**veliko**	**ve**leekoh
small	**malo**	**mah**loh
hot	**vruć**	vrooch
cold	**hladan**	**hlah**dan
good	**dobar**	**do**bar
bad	**loš**	losh
open	**otvoreno**	ot**vohr**enoh
closed	**zatvoreno**	zat**vohr**enoh
left	**lijevo**	**lee**yevoh
right	**desno**	**des**noh
straight on	**ravno**	**rav**noh
near	**blizu**	**blee**zoo
far	**daleko**	dal**e**koh
up	**gore**	**go**rey
down	**dolje**	**dol**yey

Shopping

early	**rano**	**ra**noh
late	**kasno**	**ka**snoh
entrance	**ulaz**	**oo**laz
exit	**izlaz**	**ee**zlaz
toilet	**WC**	Vey tsey
more	**više**	**vee**shey
less	**manje**	**man**yey

How much does this cost?	**Koliko ovo košta?**	**ko**likoh ovoh **ko**shta
I would like...	**Volio bih...**	**vo**lioh bee...
Do you have...?	**Imate li...?**	**ee**matey lee...
I'm just looking	**Samo gledam**	Samoh gledam
Do you take credit cards?	**Primate li kreditne kartice?**	**pree**matey lee credeetney cart**ee**tsey
What time do you open/close?	**Kad otvarate/ zatvarate?**	kad otv**ara**tey/ zatv**ara**tey
This one	**Ovaj**	**ov**-igh
That one	**Onaj**	**on**-igh
expensive	**skupo**	**skoo**poh
cheap	**jeftino**	**yef**teenoh
size (clothes)	**veličina**	vel**ee**chinah
size (shoes)	**broj**	broy
white	**bijelo**	bee**yel**oh
black	**crno**	**tsrn**oh
red	**crveno**	**tsrv**enoh
yellow	**žuto**	**zhoo**toh
green	**zeleno**	**zel**enoh
blue	**plavo**	**pla**voh
bakery	**pekara**	**pe**karah
bank	**banka**	**ban**kah
book shop	**knjižara**	**knyee**zharah
butcher's	**mesnica**	**mes**nitsah
cake shop	**slastičarna**	**slast**eecharnah
chemist's	**apoteka**	apoh**tek**ah
fishmonger's	**ribarnica**	**ree**barnitsah
market	**tržnica**	trzh**neet**sah
hairdresser's	**frizer**	**free**zer
newsagent's	**trafika**	**tra**feekah
post office	**pošta**	**posh**tah

Sightseeing

art gallery	**galerija umjetnina**	galer**ee**yah oomyetneenah
cathedral	**katedrala**	kated**ral**ah
church	**crkva**	**tsrk**vah
library	**knjižnica**	**knyee**zhneetsah
museum	**muzej**	**moo**zey
tourist information centre	**turistički ured**	too**reest**eechkey **oo**red
bus station	**autobusni kolodvor**	aooto**boos**nee **kol**odvor
railway station	**željeznički kolodvor**	**zhel**yeznichkih **kol**odvor

Staying in a Hotel

Do you have a vacant room?	**Imate li sobu?**	**ee**matey lee **so**boo
double room	**dvokrevetna soba**	**dvo**krevetnah **so**bah
single room	**jednokrevetna soba**	**yed**nokrevetnah **so**bah
room with a bath	**soba sa kupatilom**	**so**bah sah koo**pat**eelom
shower	**tuš**	toosh
I have a reservation	**Imam rezervaciju**	**ee**mam rezervatseeyoo

126

Eating Out

Have you got a table for...?	**Imate li stol za...?**	ee**mat**ey lee stol zah
I want to reserve a table	**Želim rezervirati stol**	**Zhel**eem rezen**veer**atee stol
The bill please	**Molim vas, račun**	**mol**eem vas, **ra**choon
I am	**Ja sam**	yah sam
a vegetarian	**vegeterijanac**	vegetereey**an**ats
waiter/waitress	**konobar/ konobarica**	**ko**nobar/ kono**bar**itsah
menu	**jelovnik**	**yel**ovneek
wine list	**vinska karta**	**veen**skah kartah
glass	**čaša**	**cha**shah
bottle	**boca**	**bot**sah
knife	**nož**	nozh
fork	**viljuška**	**veel**yooshkah
spoon	**žlica**	zhl**eet**sah
breakfast	**doručak**	**do**roochak
lunch	**ručak**	**roo**chak
dinner	**večera**	**vech**erah
main course	**glavno jelo**	**glav**noh yeloh
starters	**predjela**	**pred**yelah

Menu Decoder

bijela riba	bee**yelah reebah**	"white" fish
blitva	**bleet**vah	Swiss chard
brudet	broo**det**	fish stew
čevapčići	chev**ap**cheechee	meatballs
crni rižot	tsrnee reezhot	black risotto
desert	des**ert**	dessert
glavno jelo	**glav**noh **yel**oh	main course
grah	grah	beans
gulaš	**goo**lash	goulash
jastog	**yas**tog	lobster
juha	**yoo**hah	soup
kuhano	**koo**hanoh	cooked
maslinovo ulje	**mas**leenovoh **ool**yey	olive oil
meso na žaru	**mes**oh nah **zhar**oo	barbecued meat
miješano meso	meej**esh**anoh **mes**oh	mixed grilled meats
na žaru	nah **zhar**oo	barbecued
ocat	**ot**sat	vinegar
palačinke	pala**cheen**kay	pancakes
papar	**pap**ar	pepper
pečeno	**pech**enoh	baked
piletina	**peel**eteenah	chicken
plava riba	**plav**ah **reeb**ah	"blue" fish
predjelo	**pred**yeloh	starters
prilog	**pree**log	side dish
pršut	**prsh**oot	smoked ham
pržene lignje	**przh**ene **leeg**nyey	fried squid
prženo	**przh**enoh	fried
ramsteak	**ram**steyk	rump steak
ražnjići	razh**nyee**chee	pork kebabs
riba na žaru	**reeb**ah nah **zhar**oo	barbecued fish
rižot frutti di mare	**reezh**ot **froot**ee dee **mar**ey	seafood risotto
rižot sa škampima	**reezh**ot sah **shkam**peemah	scampi risotto
salata	sal**at**ah	salad
salata od hobotnice	sal**at**ah od **hob**otneetsey	octopus salad
sarma	**sar**mah	cabbage leaves
sir	seer	cheese
sladoled	**slad**oled	ice cream
slana srdela	**slan**ah srdelah	salted sardines
škampi na buzaru	**shkam**pee nah **boo**zaroo	scampi in tomato and onion
školjke na buzaru	**shkol**kay nah **boo**zaroo	shellfish in tomato and onion
špageti frutti di mare	shpa**get**ee **froot**ee dee marey	spaghetti with seafood
sol	sol	salt
tjestenina	**tjest**eneenah	pasta stuffed with meat and rice
ulje	**ool**yey	oil

Drinks

bijelo vino	bee**yeloh veenoh**	white wine
crno vino	**tsrn**oh **veen**oh	red wine
gazirana/ negazirana mineralna voda	gaze**eran**ah/ **ney**gazeeranah meener**al**nah **vod**ah	sparkling/still mineral water
čaj	ch-igh	tea
kava	**kav**ah	coffee
pivo	**pee**voh	bccr

Numbers

0	**nula**	**noo**lah
1	**jedan**	**ye**dan
2	**dva**	dvah
3	**tri**	tree
4	**četiri**	**chet**eeree
5	**pet**	pet
6	**šest**	shest
7	**sedam**	**se**dam
8	**osam**	**o**sam
9	**devet**	**de**vet
10	**deset**	**de**set
11	**jedanaest**	**ye**danest
12	**dvanaest**	**dvah**nest
13	**trinaest**	**tree**nest
14	**četrnaest**	**chet**rnest
15	**petnaest**	**pet**nest
16	**šestnaest**	**shes**nest
17	**sedamnaest**	**se**damnest
18	**osamnaest**	**o**samnest
19	**devetnaest**	**de**vetnest
20	**dvadeset**	**dvah**deset
21	**dvadeset i jedan**	**dvah**deset ee **ye**dan
30	**trideset**	**tree**deset
31	**trideset i jedan**	**tree**deset ee **ye**dan
40	**četrdeset**	**chet**rdeset
50	**pedeset**	**pe**deset
60	**šezdeset**	**shez**deset
70	**sedamdeset**	**se**damdeset
80	**osamdeset**	**o**samdeset
90	**devedeset**	**de**vedeset
100	**sto**	stoh
101	**sto i jedan**	stoh ee **ye**dan
102	**sto i dva**	stoh ee **dvah**
200	**dvjesto**	**dvee**stoh
500	**petsto**	**pet**stoh
700	**sedamsto**	**se**damstoh
900	**devetsto**	**de**vetstoh
1,000	**tisuću**	**tee**soochoo

Time

One minute	**jedan minuta**	**ye**dan mee**noo**tah
One hour	**jedan sat**	**ye**dan saht
Half an hour	**pola sata**	**pol**ah sahtah
Monday	**ponedjeljak**	pon**ed**yelyak
Tuesday	**utorak**	**oo**torak
Wednesday	**srijeda**	sree**jed**ah
Thursday	**četvrtak**	**chet**vrtak
Friday	**petak**	**pet**ak
Saturday	**subota**	**soo**botah
Sunday	**nedjelja**	**ned**yelyah

Dalmatia Map Index

This index follows Croatian alphabetical order, with Č, Š and Ž following at the end of entries for C, S and Z.